Anti-Corruption

Implementing Curriculum Change
in Management Education

ANTI-CORRUPTION

Implementing Curriculum Change in Management Education

Written by **Wolfgang Amann**, **Ronald Berenbeim**, **Tay Keong Tan**,
Matthias Kleinhempel, **Alfred Lewis**, **Ruth Nieffer**,
Agata Stachowicz-Stanusch and **Shiv Tripathi**

Greenleaf
PUBLISHING

© 2015 Greenleaf Publishing

Published by Greenleaf Publishing Limited
Aizlewood's Mill
Nursery Street
Sheffield S3 8GG
UK
www.greenleaf-publishing.com

Cover by Sadie Gornall-Jones

Printed and bound by Printondemand-worldwide.com, UK

British Library Cataloguing in Publication Data:
A catalogue record for this book is available from the British Library.

ISBN-13: 978-1-78353-473-9 [hardback]
ISBN-13: 978-1-78353-510-1 [paperback]
ISBN-13: 978-1-78353-474-6 [PDF ebook]
ISBN-13: 978-1-78353-475-3 [ePub ebook]

Contents

Figures and tables

Figures

Tables

Preface

Ronald Berenbeim
New York University Stern School of Business Administration;
Co-facilitator, PRME Working Group on Anti-Corruption

There are three key elements of a profession, which can be characterized as established criteria for: (1) admission; (2) legitimate practice; and (3) proper conduct. There is agreement in principle if not in practice that that the standard of admission for business practice ought to include an ability to recognize that corrupt behavior falls short of legitimate practice and that proper conduct requires an effective response to it. Devising an ethics and anti-corruption curriculum for global use in a business environment of actors with fundamentally different cultural, enterprise, and functional business conduct standards is the task that the Principles for Responsible Management Education (PRME) Working Group on Anti-Corruption (ACWG) has set itself.

Over a period of four years, the members of ACWG met in five venues: Copenhagen, Buenos Aires, New York, Rio de Janeiro, and Berlin. The ACWG participants are all business school faculty members, from 15 different countries, and have also taught MBA courses at many other institutions throughout the world. At the outset, the group focused on developing core subject matter for use in MBA curricula worldwide and recruited educational institutions that were willing to engage local and regional business, governmental and NGO leaders in conferences, meetings, classroom lectures, and internship programs. In so doing, the ACWG sought to create a virtuous circle of continuously improving and mutually reinforcing leadership education, research, and public engagement.

This book documents and analyzes the ACWG's efforts during the last four years. It describes challenges and successes and marks the path forward. It is an invitation to all who read it to become involved in this effort and it offers examples of how human rights, gender equity, poverty alleviation, environmental sustainability, and CSR proponents can and have made vital contributions.

Introduction

The reason we need an anti-corruption curriculum is perfectly illustrated through the recurring headlines of yet another corruption incident. Stories range from the known patterns of corruption to more innovative and creative schemes that quickly gain notoriety. In 2013, for example, an international meat scandal took consumers, retailers, and regulators by surprise. In more than a dozen countries in Europe, food that was advertised as beef product contained horsemeat – in some cases 100%. The problem was not only the improper declaration. The substantially cheaper horsemeat came from animals that were not allowed to enter the food supply chain. The veterinary drug phenylbutazone, for example, is universally banned in animals that may be used in human consumption (see Lyons, 2013). Further tests revealed that larger samples of beef products also contained standard pork, which is unacceptable and problematic in Muslim and Jewish communities. What astounded many people was the scale of the problem; the volumes of meat were considerable, and sophisticated distribution networks reached across Europe. Corrupt industry players creatively and ruthlessly circumvented established quality standards and control systems to generate monetary benefits. These players harmed established and trusted relationships.

Today's corruption challenges reach far and wide. In India, it is estimated that the damage caused by corruption surpasses the national government's budget for healthcare. In the People's Republic of China, former politician Bo Xilai, son of a founder of the Communist Party and an erstwhile promising contestant of the current Chinese president, Xi Jinping, accumulated hundreds of millions of dollars (U.S.) to supplement his official but modest monthly salary. There are examples in all countries and in many industries around the globe. They underline the necessity of exploring and strengthening the anti-corruption curriculum in business schools, which have to make a conscious decision whether to be silent partners in crime or to be the cradle of great next-generation leaders (see Gan *et al.*, 2014).

In this book and the corresponding online Toolkit (actoolkit. unprme.org), we argue that successful businesses are built on trust. Employees and colleagues need to trust one another and earn trust from customers, suppliers, and politicians who shape business environments and regulatory frameworks.

The thoughts in this book represent the collective expertise and experience of members of the Principles for Responsible Management Education (PRME) Working Group on Anti-Corruption. PRME is an initiative supported by the United Nations Global Compact with the mission to inspire and champion responsible management education, research, and thought leadership globally by bridging relationships and catalyzing collaboration among the United Nations, the Global Compact, and academia. The Six Principles of PRME are based on internationally accepted values endorsed by UN member states and provide an engagement framework for higher education institutions to embed responsibility and sustainability in education, research, and campus practices through a process of continuous improvement. Higher education institutions that become signatory to the Principles of PRME make a public commitment to knowledge creation and education that supports and develops leaders who are capable of managing the complex challenges faced by business and society in the 21st century. Like the Global Compact, PRME is a multi-stakeholder platform with a dynamic network of local and global learning communities, including thematic working groups and regional chapters, which collaborate on projects and events. Since its official launch in 2007 by UN Secretary-General Ban Ki-moon, the PRME initiative has grown to more than 600 leading business schools and management-related academic institutions from over 80 countries across the world.

The PRME Anti-Corruption Toolkit offers resources for building trust in the business world through implementing comprehensive guidelines on how to professionalize ethics and anti-corruption education worldwide in various classroom settings. It is written and tested by highly experienced program directors, deans, and professors, and it elaborates on how to adopt, adapt, and develop best teaching practice. It highlights successful patterns, details illustrative case studies, and offers clear, hands-on recommendations. The PRME Anti-Corruption Toolkit enables business schools, management-related academic institutions, and executive training programs to embed curriculum change quickly to achieve positive outcomes.

This book, along with many related initiatives, has its origin in the Siemens Integrity Initiative. Back in 2009, Siemens and the World Bank Group reached a comprehensive settlement in the aftermath of a corruption scandal in Russia in which Siemens was involved. Siemens agreed to contribute $100 million to anti-corruption initiatives over the subsequent 15 years. Siemens also agreed to the debarment of its Russian subsidiary for a period of four years and a voluntary 24-month pause from key bidding processes. This settlement catalyzes many initiatives of the World Bank and beyond when it comes to fighting corruption. The allocated $100 million should foster collective action, education, and training. Collective action in this context aims to increase compliance standards and enhance awareness through alliances between the public and private sectors. Education and training in turn build capacity, foster a culture of integrity, and promote knowledge sharing between institutions and stakeholders.

PRME, in collaboration with the UN Global Compact, set up and has been supporting an academic Working Group on Anti-Corruption (ACWG) for a period of four years. This task force aimed to integrate anti-corruption values into the core curricula of leading business schools. The project promoted ethical decision making and anti-corruption competences at the post-baccalaureate level by offering business schools and management-related academic institutions a state-of-the-art anti-corruption "Toolkit." A truly global group of expert academics joined forces to compile an integrated set of new readings, tools, exercises, and education cases. This anti-corruption curriculum is now available online free of charge at actoolkit.unprme.org. The Toolkit provides guidance and step-by-step approaches for the successful design of curricula, along with detailed methods, techniques, mechanisms, and processes for effective changes in response to management education.

Numerous pilot projects, implementing initial or revised versions of a modern anti-corruption curriculum, have been launched and finalized around the globe. Progress reports have also been made available online; the authors of the Anti-Corruption Toolkit wish to enhance support for business school deans, program directors, and involved faculty members even more. This book distills key lessons learned and success patterns, and also traps to avoid when it comes to curriculum change. It integrates insights from the progress reports, supporting implementation initiatives and experiences from leading curriculum change programs in our own organizations. It intends to accelerate the international dissemination of modern anti-corruption curricula and ensure its ongoing improvement. The following section outlines the flow of the book and the purpose and content of individual chapters. It is our hope that even the most sophisticated examples of corruption, such as the above-mentioned horsemeat scandal, will be more easily detected, prevented, and preempted by a better-trained generation of leaders and managers.

The structure of the book

This book summarizes the lessons learned from implementing the anti-corruption curriculum in various international settings, ranging from undergraduate to executive education programs.

Chapter 1 reviews a modern understanding of corruption as a phenomenon and anti-corruption initiatives in management education. As in the online Anti-Corruption Toolkit, Chapter 1 elaborates how corruption can mutate over time. It is a fluid concept on an individual and a collective level. Confucius already knew and commented on its detrimental effects, and many researchers have tried to map its cause-and-effect relationships. This is followed by a review of international initiatives to fight corruption, including Organisation for Economic Co-operation and Development (OECD) and UN activities, before outlining the Principles of PRME.

Chapter 2 continues with a presentation and discussion of experiences gathered when the Anti-Corruption Toolkit was implemented internationally. The nature and value of the Anti-Corruption Toolkit were recognized at several locations. It is best understood as a buffet of resources in the form of readings, cases, and exercises. Local deans, program directors, and professors used parts of this buffet to construct tailored learning journeys. Not all the readings, cases, or discussion questions offered online were of the same use to everybody: the online Anti-Corruption Toolkit is far too comprehensive for that. There were also efforts to localize the Anti-Corruption Toolkit, either with additional local readings, or by extending or shortening the case studies. We recommend that any program director or faculty member interested in using the Anti-Corruption Toolkit should also explore local adaptations in addition to the global overview that is offered.

Chapter 3 emphasizes the need to tailor the Anti-Corruption Toolkit further, offering various options and choices for designing local courses. Target groups in different programs and with heterogeneous levels of experience require a different selection from the rich buffet of resources. Cultures and business practices around the world differ extensively. Therefore, certain values and behaviors receive different levels of attention and merit more discussion in some settings than others. The learning goals of the programs also matter. Do they prioritize knowledge, comprehension, application, analysis, synthesis, or evaluation of corruption challenges? This also applies to different learning styles around the world. Some management education learning cultures still prefer the classic all-knowing professor and one-way communication or lecturing. Elsewhere, different methods of high-impact learning have spread. First, sufficient time is devoted to clarifying why an issue at hand is important and why time should be spent on it. This sensitizes the students or course participants to the topic. Second, a more modern way of learning brings interplay between exploring the concepts theoretically and shedding light on the practical ways in which they work. Third, there is a phase of active experimentation. At times, phases two and three may switch positions. Fourth, there is reflection on how to use the concepts in the future and in the course participants' personal contexts. Over the last decades, the weight of management education reflection has increased substantially and is an essential element of modern-day learning journeys, adding value for executives and undergraduates alike. Chapter 3 continues by describing a model curriculum as a point of orientation and reflecting on international best practice. A sample syllabus is presented in the Appendix to allow the reader to view a strong example in detail, which should help develop tailored, local solutions.

The online Anti-Corruption Toolkit deals with the following ten core issues:

1. A review of the fundamental concepts

2. Understanding economics, market failures, and professional dilemmas, including violence

3. Legislation and fiduciary duties

4. The causes of, psychological explanations for, and benefits of corruption

5. Specific forms of corruption

6. International standards and supply chain issues

7. The active management of anti-corruption initiatives

8. Organizational aspects and fighting corruption

9. Mechanisms to discover truth, enable disclosure, fostering whistleblowing, and loyalty

10. The development of a global anti-corruption compliance regime

Chapter 4 continues the learning journey by clarifying that these ten topics represent an agenda that all types of programs should cover. All ten topics cannot be integrated everywhere. Most executive education programs are too short and usually include more topics aimed at quickly making leaders and managers more effective in other fields. The time spent with customers during executive education programs is far too limited. Chapter 4 therefore outlines recommendations for how to deal with anti-corruption in executive education seminars.

Chapter 5 clarifies that the Anti-Corruption Toolkit can and should be updated with locally relevant case studies. For that to happen successfully, this chapter outlines key insights on how to rapidly compile such case studies. Cases have become core tools in the education of next-generation leaders and managers. These case studies easily complement the general readings in the Anti-Corruption Toolkit.

Chapter 6 aims to link the work of the Anti-Corruption Toolkit to the efforts and output of other PRME Working Groups. Anti-corruption education is understood as part of conveying a sound management and leadership philosophy. Being a good corporate citizen and living up to the increasing standards for social and environmental responsibilities cover more topics than just corruption because the topics should be linked. A level playing field with equal chances for all involved, for example, would probably fight poverty more effectively. Gender issues, equality, and human rights discussions must also be part of a sound management education system. Chapter 6 establishes the link with major progress achieved by colleagues in the other PRME Working Groups and suggests ways forward to build suitable anti-corruption curricula.

Chapter 7 sheds light on an additional key success factor to ensure that a modern anti-corruption curriculum is in place. Program directors and faculty members must update and localize the curriculum beyond case studies. The chapter outlines a framework for aligning the teaching and research activities in the form of an integrated value chain. As seen in the example of the horsemeat scandal, corruption is not a static phenomenon. The more the anti-corruption camp makes progress, the more creative and adaptive corrupt players seem to become. Using Nassim Taleb's (2014) terminology, corruption seems to be an "anti-fragile" phenomenon. As international frameworks evolve, corporate practices advance, and management education initiatives professionalize, corruption seems to progress competitively. More research needs to be done on corruption and how anti-corruption efforts might contribute. The chapter outlines how synergies can be created to advance our body of knowledge on corruption as well as on anti-corruption initiatives.

Chapter 8 presents future perspectives on using the Anti-Corruption Toolkit in business schools. One way forward lies in far more productive cooperation between academia and business, whether in the form of joint research centers, creating best-practice platforms, innovative training formats that leverage those currently used to make progress, collective action in the form of joint projects, or co-creating new solutions to be jointly implemented, to name but a few examples.

This should, however, not shift the core responsibilities away from business schools. Business schools fulfill a variety of functions for society, companies, and individuals. They ought to supply the labor market with a next generation of talent that can cope with the complexity of the corruption phenomenon. Creating value without compromising values should be a skill that future graduates can master, even more than in the past. In turn, individuals often expect business schools to be a character gym in which they develop not only their business acumen but also personality. Maintaining an up-to-date anti-corruption curriculum, which is locally adapted, is a major step forward.

This book continues with a review of the corruption phenomenon and summarizes the content of the Anti-Corruption Toolkit. It offers a comprehensive collection of resources from which readers can select their own approaches. We encourage the reader to start with those topics that are most relevant and urgent.

References

Gan, N., Zhou, L. & Meng, A. (2014, December 23). Luxury French villa of jailed Chinese politician Bo Xilai "up for sale at HK$66 million." *South China Morning Post*. Retrieved from www.scmp.com/news/china/article/1667708/luxury-french-villa-jailed-chinese-politician-bo-xilai-sale-hk66-million on April 21, 2015.

Lyons, J. (2013, January 24). Contamination fear: Cancer-causing drug could be in burgers, consumers warned. *Mirror*. Retrieved from www.mirror.co.uk/news/uk-news/horsemeat-scandal-cancer-causing-drug-phenylbuta-zone-1553043 on April 21, 2015.

Taleb, N. (2014). *Antifragile: Things that Gain from Disorder (Incerto)*. New York, NY: Routledge.

1
Understanding corruption, anti-corruption and anti-corruption initiatives in management education

The following chapter summarizes the essence of the available body of knowledge on corruption and anti-corruption initiatives. It begins with a review of the definitions, which is where the complexity of the phenomenon starts. Converging toward one definition is challenging, as corruption relates to individuals, as well as at group or organization level – both of which need different models and remedies. The chapter continues with the negative effects of corruption. International initiatives are reviewed before the chapter closes with remarks on the role of management education.

1.1 Defining corruption

Corruption is a global phenomenon that exists in a variety of forms. Its mutating forms often make it difficult to identify. Corruption literature has studied the problem from local, regional, and international perspectives, and in all organizational sectors – business, charitable, nongovernmental, and governmental. In his statement on corruption, Confucius said, "authority is seductive and, in the end, causes ruination" (Letowska, 1997).

There is no universal definition of corruption, but a few perspectives can be used for this discussion. Corruption can be at either the individual or the collective level, depending on who benefits from the corrupt act (Voliotis, 2011).

There are as many definitions of corruption as there are studies that have been devoted to its research, while still not converging toward a main way of understanding it.

Alemann (1989, p. 858) says that corruption, "while being tied particularly to bribery, is a general term covering misuse of authority as a result of considerations of personal gain, which need not be monetary."

Corruption is the use of incentives, such as gifts or money to induce certain benefits or advantages, by individuals, organizations, and governmental agencies. Illegal and unethical power and domination are typically evident in the practice of corruption (Rendtorff, 2009).

Klitgaard *et al.* (2000, p. 31) state that "corruption is a crime of economic calculation. If the probability of being caught is small and the penalty is mild and pay-off is large relative to the positive incentives facing the government official, then we will tend to find corruption."

Vargas-Hernandez (2009) classifies corrupt acts as bribery, collusion, embezzlement of public funds, and theft, fraud, extortion, abuse of discretion, favoritism, clientelism, nepotism, the sale of government property by public officials, patronage, and other forms. Corruption is further classified into three groups: political corruption, economic corruption, and public administration corruption.

Several studies have addressed corruption from organizational and individual perspectives (see Pinto *et al.*, 2008). Individual analysis associates corruption with individuals or small groups. The contributing factors include lack of integrity (Frost and Rafilson, 1989), moral identity (Aquino and Reed, 2002), self-control (Marcus and Schuler, 2004), empathy (Eisenberg, 2000), low levels of cognitive moral development (Treviño 1986), or even a diagnosable psychopathology (Babiak and Hare, 2006; Bakan, 2004; Levine, 2005).

The organizational perspective directly addresses how corrupt practices and activities become engrained within organizations – thus becoming "part and parcel of everyday organizational life" (Brief *et al.*, 2001, p. 473). The organizational behavior perspective indicates that corrupt behavior within organizations is particularly influenced by situational scenarios. Depersonalized roles have essentially become the reality of organizational life; corrupt actions can therefore become institutionalized in situational instances. Behavior can be motivated and influenced by one's own identity and, as such, well-meaning individuals may engage in corrupt practices in the fulfillment of their organizational roles (Misangyi *et al.*, 2008).

According to Cragg (1998),

> corruption is any attempt, whether successful or not, to persuade someone in a position of responsibility to make a decision or recommendation on any grounds other than the intrinsic merits of the case with a view to the advantage or advancement of him – or herself or another person or group to which he or she is linked through personal commitment,

obligation, or employment, or individual, professional, or group loyalty (p. 651).

Corruption is the use of public office for private gain (Bardhan, 1997; Kaufmann, 1997). The World Bank has adopted this definition in spite of the limitation in scope and given that corruption exists beyond the public arena.

Aguilera and Vadera (2008, p. 433) define corruption as an "abuse of authority for personal benefit" and organizational corruption is defined as "the crime that is committed by the use of authority within organizations for personal gain."

Pedersen and Johannsen (2008) developed a typology of corruption based on actor categories as depicted in Table 1.1. They subdivided corruption into two broad categories of petty and grand corruption, and identified the party and counter-party involved in the scheme.

		The purchaser	The provider
Petty corruption	Day-to-day corruption	Individual citizens	Individual providers of public services – health personnel, police
	Administrative malpractice	Individual economic actors – firms, etc.	Public control and licensing agencies
Grand corruption	Political state capture	Collective economic actors – interest organizations Individual economic actors	Politicians – individuals and political parties

TABLE 1.1   A typology of corruption based on actor categories
Source: Pedersen and Johannsen (2008).

The Pedersen and Johannsen typology differentiates between "petty" corruption, observed in the junior ranks of the administrative strata and pertaining to practices that are essential for completing administrative tasks, and "grand" corruption, which occurs in the middle and senior level of public administration and distorts appropriate democratic decisions and decision-making processes. The authors assert that grand corruption is closely linked to the specific context of transforming and redefining private–public relations in society at large.

Ashforth *et al.* (2008) assert that unethical behavior and corruption stem from a complex multilevel interaction at the individual, group, and organizational levels. Thus, when examined from a micro viewpoint, corruption can be understood from the individual perspective. A lack of integrity or other psychopathological states are responsible for corruption at the individual level.

In summary, academic research has not produced a single, universally used definition. This is why each researcher, faculty member, or program director must spend time clarifying what is truly at the center of the debate. The chapter continues with a critical review of corruption's negative impact.

1.2 Negative effect of corruption

According to Ouzounov (2004), corruption at the local, national, and international level is a global challenge, because of its collateral effects of suboptimal governance, retardation of social development, and widespread poverty due to diminished economic growth and income distribution effects (Banerjee *et al.*, 2006).

Corruption is also destructive due to its negative effects on the underprivileged population: it benefits a small group while a large majority is deprived of access to rudimentary social services, education, healthcare, affordable housing, and public transportation.

Corruption can also be examined from the corporate social responsibility (CSR) perspective, which ultimately wishes to enhance/engender ethical and responsible conduct by corporations. Traditionally, CSR research has been focused on bad corporate practices, such as complicity in human rights abuses, pollution, environmental exploitation, and their related negative consequences (Terracino, 2007). These are "externalities" that can add to the cost of doing business. For this reason, there are synergies between sound CSR practices and reduced levels of corruption through the promotion of more positive corporate and individual conduct.

The most corrupt countries generally have low income levels, distorted market structures, restriction in their market and political competition, and reduced public and private investments, as well as overall inflows of foreign direct investment (Wei, 2000).

The 2008 global economic meltdown can be traced in part to financial-sector corruption (Teather, 2009; Voliotis, 2011; Watkins, 2003). According to a report by the World Bank (2000), corruption is a major impediment for economic and social development. A study by Aguilera and Vadera (2008) suggests that corruption has existed for a long time. Thus the goal is to institute practices and systems that will help prevent corruption and that are based on transparency principles. Only then will we see improvements over time. There are numerous examples of such practices and systems in the governmental sector and for-profit organizations throughout the world.

Given the contextual nature in which employees act in organizations, other studies are based on the ethical climate theory. ECT was initially discussed by Victor and Cullen (1987, 1988), who defined organizational ethical climate as the organization's "shared perceptions of what is ethically correct behavior and how ethical issues should be handled" (Victor and Cullen, 1987, pp. 51–52). The theory provides a framework to better understand the effects of bullying in the workplace, behavioral ethics, job satisfaction, and organizational commitment.

According to Wankel (2009, p. 54),

> organizations and societies recognize that ethically and socially responsible behavior is a crucial underpinning of good business practice. This realization is leading employers around the world to expect and demand that business schools train students in ethics and social responsibility. Research, however, is mixed on how well business schools are responding to these pressures.

Krehmeyer (2007) found that a significant number of management schools were not building their programs on a basis grounded in ethics. Cheating is not uncommon in business schools. It can thus be inferred that such unethical behaviors by business/management students have an impact on society overall (Shin and Harman, 2009). Tang *et al.* (2008) found that management students tend to engage in greed, Machiavellianism, and associated unethical behaviors. A study by Wilson (2008) reported that many business students are misguided in the belief that their unethical behavior is justified because their peers are also unethical.

Given the ever-increasing global interconnectedness due to technological advances, management education needs to include training to diminish corrupt practices in organizations. The legal system addresses corruption after the fact, whereas the management education goal is to reduce corruption through ethical practices and systems that reduce the moral hazard risk. There are several efforts underway aimed at addressing corruption.

1.3 International initiatives

1.3.1 The OECD Convention on Combating Bribery of Foreign Public Officials in International Business Transactions (OECD Convention)

The OECD Convention (1997) is recognized as the most significant anti-corruption initiative. It established legally binding standards to criminalize the offering of bribes to foreign public officials during international business transactions and it also includes mechanisms to ensure compliance. The standards are not legally binding, but each country is charged with establishing individual standards with the framework of the Convention (IMF 2001).

The 34 OECD member countries, along with seven non-member countries (Argentina, Brazil, Bulgaria, Colombia, Latvia, Russia, and South Africa) have adopted the Convention. In these countries, the bribery of foreign public officials is illegal and they agree to submit their legal frameworks and enforcement efforts for review. The OECD Working Group on Bribery in International Business Transactions, which is composed of representatives of all the Convention signatories, conducts the individual country reviews in two steps based on the complementary systems of self and mutual evaluation.

The first step is a comprehensive assessment of the extent to which the country's antibribery laws conform to the OECD Convention. The second step involves one week of meetings with ranking officials from government, law enforcement, corporations, trade unions, and civil society in the country being reviewed. Based on input from these diverse segments, the Working Group determines the effectiveness of the country's anti-foreign bribery laws.

1.3.2 The United Nations Convention against Corruption (UN Convention)

The UN Convention against Corruption was adopted by the General Assembly on October 31, 2002, and took effect in December 2005.

The UN Convention, which has been signed by 140 countries, is under the jurisdiction of the United Nations Office on Drugs and Crime (UNODC). The UNODC's role is to provide countries with assistance, in addition to helping build the required technical capacity needed to implement the Convention. The Convention covers the following four main areas: prevention, criminalization, international cooperation, and asset recovery (UNODC, 2004).

Prevention. The signatories are required to

> develop and implement or maintain effective, coordinated anti-corruption policies and to establish and promote effective practices aimed at the prevention of corruption (Art 5, UN Convention). They are also to establish anti-corruption bodies (Art 6) and enhanced transparency in the financing of election campaigns and political parties (Art 7). States must endeavor to ensure that their public services are subject to safeguards that promote efficiency, transparency and recruitment based on merit (Arts 7 & 8). Transparency and accountability in matters of public finance (Art 9) must also be promoted, and specific requirements are established for judiciary (Art 11) and public procurement (Art 9). Preventing public corruption also requires an effort from all members of society at large. For these reasons, the Convention calls on countries to promote actively the involvement of non-governmental and community-based organizations, as well as other elements of civil society, and to raise public awareness in regard to corruption and its prevention (Art 13) (UNODC, 2004).

Criminalization. The signatories must prosecute criminal and other offences covering a wide range of acts of corruption, if they are not already crimes under domestic law. In certain instances, countries are legally obliged to establish legislation in other instances, so as to account for differences in domestic law. The UN Convention is comprehensive in that it goes beyond previous agreements by criminalizing bribery and the embezzlement of public funds, such as trading in influence (Art 18), abuse of functions by public officials (Art 19), the concealment (Art 24) and "laundering" of the proceeds of corruption (Art 23). Transgressions committed in support of corruption, including money laundering (Art 23) and obstructing justice (Art 25), are also included. The Convention likewise addresses private-sector corruption (Arts 12 & 21).

International cooperation. The parties to the Convention are required to work together in every dimension of the global fight against corruption: (1) prevention, (2) investigation, and (3) prosecuting offenders (Chapter IV, UN Convention).

Asset recovery. The Convention includes asset recovery and this provision is "a fundamental principle of the Convention" (Art 51). The UN views this point as important, especially in poorer nations, due to high-level corruption where resources are needed for development.

1.3.3 UN Global Compact

The UN Global Compact extended the UN Convention and is an initiative to provide a policy platform and a practical framework for corporations committed to sustainability and principles for ethical business conduct. This initiative has been widely endorsed by corporate leaders in order to align business practices on the basis of its Ten Principles, which cover human rights, labor, the environment, and anti-corruption. As stated by the Global Compact,

> never before in history has there been a greater alignment between the objectives of the international community and those of the business world. Common goals, such as building markets, combating corruption, safeguarding the environment and ensuring social inclusion, have resulted in unprecedented partnerships and openness between business, governments, civil society, labour and the United Nations (UN Global Compact, 2008).

The Global Compact is recognized as the most extensive corporate citizenship and sustainability initiative. From the official launch on July 26, 2000, the effort has increased to involve more than 12,000 participants, including over 8,000 businesses worldwide in over 160 countries.[1] The business case for anti-corruption is based on its cost. Several studies have estimated that corruption accounts for about 5% of the global gross domestic product (U.S.$2.6 trillion) composed of U.S.$1 trillion directly attributed to bribes (El-Sharkawy *et al.*, 2006). It is estimated that corruption adds up to 10% to global business costs, and up to 25% to the cost of procurement contracts in developing countries (ICC *et al.*, n.d.). The Global Compact's Tenth Principle against corruption states that "businesses should work against corruption in all its forms, including extortion and bribery."

Another offshoot of the Global Compact is the Multi-Stakeholder Dialogue Networks Initiative to promote private–public collaboration on anti-corruption issues. The expansion of these networks at the local level is designed to aid the promotion of trust and cooperation with a variety of stakeholders with

---

1 https://www.unglobalcompact.org/what-is-gc/participants.

the ultimate goal of increasing transparency, especially between public procurements and companies that bid on these projects (Brinkmann-Braun and Pies 2007; Roloff 2008).

1.4 Conclusion: management education initiatives

Most management schools offer ethics teaching, either integrated with other classes or as a stand-alone course. A study by Christensen *et al.* (2007) reported that 84% of the MBA programs at the 50 top-ranked business schools in the world (according to the *Financial Times* ranking) have an ethics component in the curriculum, either as an independent class or combined with sustainability components. A movement appears to be underway to integrate ethics across the undergraduate and graduate curricula.

There has been an increased demand to equip management students better by providing a grounding in ethics, as well as in CSR, due to the many global scandals, especially those related to corporate practices.

To assist management education institutions in developing ethics, anti-corruption, and CSR curricula, the UN Global Compact started the PRME initiative, which aims to inspire and promote responsible management education, research, and thought leadership globally. To date, PRME has over 600 business schools and management education institutions from 80 countries that are signatories to its Principles. PRME is a set of Six Principles[2] intended to help institutes of higher education structure

2 www.unprme.org/about-prme/the-six-principles.php.

management and business programs with a special emphasis on CSR in the areas of teaching, research, and campus policies:

> Principle 1 | Purpose: We will develop the capabilities of students to be future generators of sustainable value for business and society at large and to work for an inclusive and sustainable global economy.
>
> Principle 2 | Values: We will incorporate into our academic activities and curricula the values of global social responsibility as portrayed in international initiatives such as the United Nations Global Compact.
>
> Principle 3 | Method: We will create educational frameworks, materials, processes and environments that enable effective learning experiences for responsible leadership.
>
> Principle 4 | Research: We will engage in conceptual and empirical research that advances our understanding about the role, dynamics, and impact of corporations in the creation of sustainable social, environmental and economic value.
>
> Principle 5 | Partnership: We will interact with managers of business corporations to extend our knowledge of their challenges in meeting social and environmental responsibilities and to explore jointly effective approaches to meeting these challenges.
>
> Principle 6 | Dialogue: We will facilitate and support dialogue and debate among educators, students, business, government, consumers, media, civil society organisations and other interested groups and stakeholders on critical issues related to global social responsibility and sustainability.[3]

Ultimately, the goal is to help train and develop responsible managers, which in turn will address the challenges that corrupt practices cause. A better-trained group of graduates will be able to cope more easily with corruption's challenges.

---

3 www.unprme.org/about-prme/the-six-principles.php.

References

Aguilera, R.V., & Vadera, A.K. (2008). The dark side of authority: Antecedents, mechanisms, and outcomes of organizational corruption. *Journal of Business Ethics*, 77(4), pp. 431-449.

Alemann, Ulrich von (1989). Bureaucratic and political corruption controls: Reassessing the German record. In A.J. Heidenheimer, M. Johnston, & V.T. LeVine (Eds.) *Political Corruption: A Handbook* (pp. 855-869). New Brunswick, NJ: Transaction.

Aquino, K., & Reed, A. (2002). The self-importance of moral identity. *Journal of Personality and Social Psychology*, 83, pp. 1423-1440.

Ashforth, B., Gioia, D., Robinson, S., & Treviño, L. (2008) Re-viewing organizational corruption. *Academy of Management Review*, 33(3), pp. 670-684.

Babiak, P., & Hare, R.D. (2006). *Snakes in suits: When psychopaths go to work*. New York: Harper Collins.

Bakan, J. 2004. *The Corporation: The Pathological Pursuit of Profit and Power*. New York: Free Press.

Banerjee, A.V., Benabou, R., & Mookherjee, D. (2006). *Understanding poverty*. Oxford, UK: Oxford University Press.

Bardhan, P.K. (1997). Corruption and development: A review of issues. *Journal of Economic Literature*, 35(3), pp. 1320-1346.

Brief, A.P., Buttram, R.T., & Dukerich, J.M. (2001). Collective corruption in the corporate world: Toward a process model. In: M.E. Turner (Ed.), *Groups at Work: Theory and Research*. Mahwah, NJ: Lawrence Erlbaum Associates.

Brinkmann-Braun, J., & Pies, I. (2007) *The Global Compact's Contribution to Global Governance Revisited*. Halle, Germany: Martin-Luther-Universität Halle-Wittenberg.

Christensen, L.J., Peirce, E., Hartman, L.P., Hoffman, W.M., & Carrier, J. (2007). Ethics, CSR, and sustainability in the Financial Times Top 50 Global Business Schools: Baseline data and future research directions. *Journal of Business Ethics*, 73, pp. 347-368.

Cornelius, N., Wallace, J., & Tassabehji, R. (2007). An analysis of corporate social responsibility, corporate identity, and ethics teaching in business schools. *Journal of Business Ethics*, 76, pp. 117-135.

Cragg, A.W. (1998) Business, globalization, and the logic and ethics of corruption. *International Journal*, 53(4).

Eisenberg, N. (2000). Emotion, regulation, and moral development. *Annual Review of Psychology*, 51, pp. 665-697.

El-Sharkawy, A., Jarvis, M., & Petkoski, D. (2006). *Towards a More Systematic Fight Against Corruption: The Role of the Private Sector.* New York: World Bank and World Bank Institute.

Frost, A.G., & Rafilson, F.M. (1989). Overt integrity tests versus personality-based measures and delinquency: An empirical comparison. *Journal of Business and Psychology*, 3, pp. 269-277.

ICC (International Chamber of Commerce), Transparency International, United Nations Global Compact &World Economic Forum Partnering Against Corruption Initiative (n.d.). *Clean Business is Good Business. The Business Case against Corruption.* Authors. Retrieved from www.weforum.org/pdf/paci/BusinessCaseAgainstCorruption.pdf on 26 June 2015.

IMF (International Monetary Fund) (2001, September). *OECD Convention on Combating Bribery of Foreign Public Officials in International Business Transactions.* Washington, DC: Author.

Kaufmann, D. (1997) Corruption: The facts. *Foreign Policy*, 107, pp. 114-131.

Klitgaard, R., MacLean-Abaroa, R., Parris H.L. (2000). *Corrupt Cities: A Practical Guide to Cure and Prevention*, Oakland, CA: Institute for Contemporary Studies.

Krehmeyer, D. (2007, October 26). Teaching business ethics: A critical need. *Business Week* (Online). (October 26). Retrieved from www.businessweek.com/bschools/content/oct2007/bs20071025_096141.htm on March 14, 2015.

Letowska, E. (1997). Dobro Wspólne – władza – korupcja. In E. Popławska (Ed.), *Dobro Wspólne. Władza. Korupcja. Konflikt interesów w życiu publicznym*. Warszawa: Instytut Spraw Publicznych, Centrum Konstytucjonalizmu i Kultury Prawnej.

Levine, D.P. (2005). The corrupt organization. *Human Relations*, 58(6).

Marcus, B., & Schuler, H. (2004). Antecedents of counterproductive behavior at work: A general perspective. *Journal of Applied Psychology*, 89: 647-660.

Misangyi, V.F., Weaver, G.R., & Elms, H. (2008). Ending corruption: The interplay among institutional logics, and institutional entrepreneurs. *Academy of Management Review*, 33, pp. 750-770.

Ouzounov, N.A. (2004). Facing the challenge: Corruption, state capture and the role of multinational business. *The John Marshall Law Review*, 37(4), pp. 1181-1204.

Pedersen, K.H., & Johannsen, L. (2008, May 19–21). *Corruption: Commonality, Causes and Consciences. Comparing 15 Ex-Communist Countries.* Paper prepared for the 13th NISPAcee Annual Conference, Moscow, Russia.

Pinto, J., Leana, C.R., & Pil, F.K. (2008). Corrupt organizations or organizations of corrupt individuals? Two types of organization-level corruption. *Academy of Management Review*, 33, pp. 685-709.

Rendtorff, J.D. (2009). *Responsibility, Ethics and Legitimacy of Corporations.* Copenhagen: Copenhagen Business School Press.

Roloff, J. (2008) A life cycle model of multi-stakeholder networks. *Business Ethics: A European Review*, 17, pp. 311-325.

Shin, J.C. & Harman, G. (2009). New challenges for higher education: Global and Asia-Pacific perspectives. *Asia Pacific Education Review*, 10(1), pp. 1-13.

Tang, T.L.P., Chen, Y.J., & Sutarso, T. (2008). Bad apples in bad (business) barrels: The love of money, Machiavellianism, risk tolerance, and unethical behavior. *Management Decision*, 46(1-2), pp. 243-263.

Teather, D. (2009, June 30) Bernard Madoff receives maximum 150 year sentence, *The Guardian*, [online].

Terracino, J.B. (2007) Anti-corruption: The enabling CSR principle, PhD candidate, Graduate Institute of International Studies, Geneva.

Treviño, L.K. (1986). Ethical decision making in organizations: A person-situation interactionist model. *Academy of Management Review*, 11, pp. 601-617.

UN Global Compact (2008). *United Nations Global Compact: Corporate Citizenship in the World Economy.* New York, NY: Author.

UNODC (United Nations Office on Drugs and Crime) (2004). *United Nations Convention Against Corruption.* Vienna, Austria: Author.

Vargas-Hernandez, J.G. (2009). The multiple faces of corruption: Typology, forms and levels. In A. Stachowicz-Stanusch (Ed.). *Organizational Immunity to Corruption: Building Theoretical and Research Foundations.* Warsaw: Polish Academy of Sciences.

Victor, B., & Cullen, J. (1987). A theory and measure of ethical climate in organizations. In W.C. Fredrick & L. Preston (Eds.), *Research in Corporate Social Performance and Policy* (pp. 51-71). London: JAI.

Victor, B., & Cullen, J. (1988). The organizational bases of ethical work climates. *Administrative Science Quarterly*, 33, pp. 101-125.

Voliotis, S. (2011). Abuse of ministerial authority, systemic perjury, and obstruction of justice: corruption in the shadows of organizational practice. *Journal of Business Ethics*, 102(4), pp. 537-562.

Wankel, C. (2009) Orienting business students to navigate the shoals of corruption in practice, In A. Stachowicz-Stanusch (Ed.). *Organizational Immunity to Corruption: Building Theoretical and Research Foundations.* Warsaw: Polish Academy of Sciences.

Watkins, S.S. (2003). Ethical conflicts at Enron: Moral responsibility in corporate capitalism. *California Management Review,* 45(4), pp. 6-19.

Wei, J. (2000). How taxing is corruption on international investors? Review of Economics and Statistics, 82(1), pp. 1-11.

Wilson, B.A. (2008). Predicting intended unethical behavior of business students. *Journal of Education for Business,* 83(4), pp. 187.

World Bank (2000, November). *Reforming Public Institutions and Strengthening Governance.* Washington, DC: Public Sector Group, Poverty Reduction and Economic Management Network, World Bank.

2
International experiences

Mainstream management education is based on a curricular design oriented toward learning outcomes that are defined by different stakeholder groups. Yet when it comes to the balance between educating for the larger societal good and the immediate needs of the enterprises that will buy the product (i.e., hire the graduates), the latter tends to take priority in the design and delivery of management education. Despite general agreement on the central role of integrity in management education, the education process seems to ill-prepare executives to cope effectively with the challenges of leading with integrity in a global stakeholder environment. Furthermore, relatively little is known about how management education can equip managers to cope with such challenges.

The PRME Working Group on Anti-Corruption piloted the Anti-Corruption Toolkit across selected business schools to ensure stakeholders' participation in the mainstreaming of anti-corruption and integrity education in management degree programs, and also because of its belief in the statement that a prepared mind favors ethical behavior.

This chapter explores the practical issues identified when piloting the Anti-Corruption Toolkit. It also includes reflections on implementation issues in mainstreaming anti-corruption and integrity education in business and management education, and it offers recommendations for the effective use of the Toolkit in the curriculum. Finally, it highlights strategies for making an anti-corruption and integrity curriculum dynamic and current by linking it to executive education and research processes.

2.1 Initial experience from India

In India, the Toolkit was piloted at Bangalore University's Canara Bank School of Management Studies (CBSMS), one of the country's largest low-cost management education providers. The university offers an MBA through its main campus and other affiliated business schools. It is important to note that the curriculum outline is designed centrally by the university and is common in all the affiliated business schools. The examination and assessment process is also coordinated centrally; consequently, the affiliated institutions have relatively less freedom in designing and delivering programs. In order to ensure the effective adaptation of the Toolkit to the context-specific needs, CBSMS and PRME jointly planned a series of activities in India during 2012–2014 involving different stakeholder groups. The main objectives of the pilot phase at CBSMS included: creating awareness among the key stakeholder groups (students, faculty members, program managers, institutional policymakers, chief executives, etc.) of the PRME Anti-Corruption Toolkit objectives and action plan; assessing the stakeholders' degree of preparedness for piloting the anti-corruption curriculum; determining the context-specific subject issues that needed to be addressed while preparing the curriculum; and identifying the major challenges of piloting the curriculum effectively. Based on a series of discussions, workshops, and meetings with the different stakeholder groups, the courses/modules on issues such as decision making, organization behavior, business ethics, corporate law, corporate governance, procurement and supply chain management, strategic management, business environment, marketing management, and human resource management were selected to teach anti-corruption in the master's-level management education program.

2.2 Initial experience from Tanzania

In Tanzania, the Toolkit was introduced at Mzumbe University through its School of Business. The process started with a faculty orientation workshop followed by stakeholder meetings. In Tanzania, master's-level business education is usually provided through a combination of course work and research, which offered a unique opportunity to extend the Toolkit for research. The Toolkit contents were implemented in different programs at master's and bachelor's level, providing wider scope for testing the suitability across the different types of programs. During the Tanzanian piloting, the Toolkit's use in short-term executive education was also tested through three different collaborative anti-corruption and ethics training programs organized in partnership with other public-sector institutions.

In Tanzania, the curriculum was also tested for an open-enrollment executive course. Executive education is critical in the management education process because it offers direct linkage to convert learning into action and, in so doing, helps reshape management-related knowledge content through real-time feedback. Executive education is often generalized across contexts owing to similarities in user characteristics. However, in practice there is a great deal of variation due to change in the context. These variations become important in ethics and anti-corruption programs, as the profiles, industries, and experience of the executives in a given context greatly influence issues such as content, pedagogy, and duration. During the piloting of the Anti-Corruption Toolkit in executive programs in Tanzania, we tested the Toolkit with different types of organization.

The school organized a training program for anti-corruption officials in Tanzania, focusing on recent development in global corporate laws and on how the conventional roles of regulatory bodies and government officials are changing on curbing corruption processes. We also designed a program for local police officials, focusing more on behavioral issues relating to corruption, including training on ethical and unethical behavior. These programs focused mainly on initial efforts to create partnerships for collaborative learning and development. Collaboration with public-sector institutions was particularly emphasized in the executive training process, as this offered great support for preparing for the next steps with a longer-term focus. Further, given the relatively smaller capacity of business schools in developing countries, the collective approach generated synergy across institutions.

During the second year of the Toolkit implementation, we partnered the Procurement and Supplies Professionals and Technician Board (PSPTB) to deliver a joint program on ethics compliance and prevention of corruption in Tanzanian corporations. The program participants provided good leads to further context-specific knowledge development on the subject. The training needs of the different executive groups also varied greatly, depending on a number of factors, such as the program focus, the role of shorter executive education assignments, and a school's ability to integrate normative management into its curriculum. We found it useful to create synergy through local partnerships. This PSPTB partnership helped us attract the right trainees and link the training program to context-specific functional needs. In the future, the PSPTB partnership will be a key element, because it is the professional body responsible for setting the ethical practice standards in procurement and supply management. This partnership's interventions through the adoption of suggested models or frameworks will be helpful for effective Toolkit training.

During the Tanzania piloting, we tested the Toolkit in different ways for use in research. The Toolkit was used as a reference book, comprising the latest resources on anti-corruption and related issues. This helped to develop a scientific research concept for a dissertation on anti-corruption practices in a multinational consulting firm in Tanzania. The Toolkit was helpful with identifying the resources related to the topic and served as a potential one-stop anti-corruption and management reference book for the research. However, in order to ensure its relevance as a potential research resource, the Toolkit requires regular modification and updating with primary and secondary research.

Executive education also helps improve context-specific resources through knowledge sharing by practicing professionals during training programs (see Figure 2.1). This effect was observed during an executive training program organized for procurement and supply management professionals in Tanzania. During the training sessions, the participants were encouraged to share the dilemmas and scenarios that they faced while struggling with corruption issues in their organizations. After an initial discussion, the participants were provided with the template that aimed to capture the potential local issues in the management of anti-corruption processes. The responses highlighted the critical dilemmas in Tanzanian organizations' procurement and supply management. These resources can be further developed and classified according their scope and relevance.

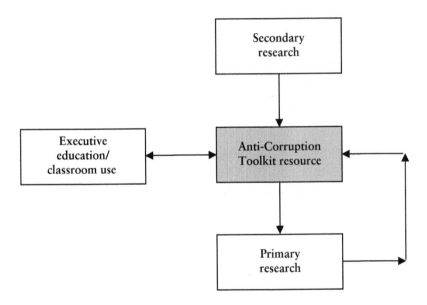

FIGURE 2.1 Possible research interface for dynamic and customized Anti-Corruption Toolkit

Indian and Tanzanian experience demonstrates that with careful alignment, the Anti-Corruption Toolkit can also be used as a primary research resource. The primary research output can be used as new Toolkit input knowledge, which, depending on the material's methodology, scope, and coverage, can be positioned at an appropriate level for further dissemination. The regular bringing together of the Toolkit with the training modules also helps to capture dilemmas or scenarios that can be edited for Toolkit use. This unique potential to co-create knowledge with training and research makes this Toolkit a wonderful dynamic resource with the scope to incorporate customized knowledge.

Based on the experiences of Toolkit use in the research process, the following are recommendations for its further application:

1. Students can use the Toolkit as a research reference resource. This will not only help to link issues to the context-specific realities, but will also provide a basis for further discussion and investigation.

2. The use of the Toolkit in training sessions will encourage participant knowledge sharing. The moderators or facilitators can design templates in advance to capture the required input, which can be further edited and selectively incorporated into the Toolkit.

3. Secondary research can enrich the Toolkit content once the participating institutions have done the initial screening and obtained approval in consultation with the appropriate PRME Working Group on Anti-Corruption team.

4. There is no single standard for Toolkit use. The participants are encouraged to use this resource for innovation provided that the teaching and research objectives are in line with the intended application.

2.3 Experience from Poland

The Silesian University of Technology (POLSL) has an almost 70-year history as an important public culture and opinion-forming institution, deeply rooted in the city of Gliwice and the Upper Silesia region. The university is the region's biggest technical university and one of Poland's largest. It has approximately 30,000 students and 14 faculties. POLSL is one of the 12 business schools that participated in the Toolkit pilot phase.

POLSL used the Anti-Corruption Toolkit for a course on The Nature and Prevention of Corrupt Behaviors within an Organization. The Toolkit was used for the course and content design. It also pointed the faculty toward new, more efficient educational methods in subjects such as anti-corruption management, ethics in the organizational behavioral context, and corporate social responsibility. The use of case studies facilitated a multilevel review of the ethical dilemmas present in contemporary organizations. In their analyses, the students discussed corrupt activity, the business objectives of corrupt behavior, and the threat that corruption in the community poses to business activity within a company. The analyzed cases were considered from ethical, legal, and business (including economic effectiveness) standpoints, from the perspective of a single actor in corrupt processes (worker, manager, or government employee) and from that of the wider group of stakeholders (entire enterprises, individual sectors, and society). During discussions, the different cultural contexts presented in many of the case studies made it difficult to understand individual motives for the action in the situations discussed, and, many students searched for analogies and references to local Polish conditions. We therefore decided to develop case studies that would better fit Polish conditions and culture, and involved the students in this process. Their engagement in the subject included:

- The choice of a few most widely commented on and interesting cases of corruption scandals that had occurred in Poland during the last decade

- The preparation and description of a case study covering the following issues:

  - The course of events in the corruption incident

  - The causes of the corruption

  - The actions taken against the corruption

  - The social response

  - The legal consequences and other sanctions

  - The results

- The use of contrasting case studies in class discussions of prevention mechanisms

The students constructed five well-developed case studies of Polish corruption scandals:

- "Skin hunters" – which documented emergency hospital staff's sale of information about deaths ("skins" in the jargon) to local funeral companies

- "The Miroslaw G. affair" – about corruption in the medical environment; specifically, the case of a surgeon (Miroslaw G.) accused of bribery to avoid a shortage of blood at that time

- "The salt scandal" – which involved a chemical company selling industrial salt (a byproduct of chemical processing) to food companies, which reduced their costs by using it as cooking salt

- "The petrol mob" – fraud and corruption in the petroleum industry involving not only business people but also police in an effort to combat local resistance to pipelines and pollution

- "Rywingate" – a scandal about corruption and illegal lobbying focused on media law; the main suspect was a well-known Polish film producer (Lew Rywin). In exchange for a bribe of US$17.5 million, Rywin offered to arrange a change in a draft law that would limit the print media's influence on radio and television

Discussion of the above cases was enhanced by additional activities. The students were asked to provide a visual artifact or movie that would popularize anti-corruption attitudes focused on the case study material. The students produced T-shirts, cups, posters, and short movies. These were distributed to the academic community as examples of viral marketing.

Inspired by our students, we hope to use the set of well-developed case studies in our future discussions and lectures on anti-corruption behavior and to describe other cases, not only of scandals, but also of effective Polish anti-corruption practices. Additionally, some of the prepared cases can be used in other Eastern European business schools currently preparing their students to confront similar business and cultural challenges in their professional careers.

The Polish stakeholders were enthusiastic about the prospect of integrating the Toolkit materials into the mainstream business education curriculum. They also stressed a need for partnerships between businesses, nongovernmental organizations, and community organizations to develop and deliver relevant course material for anti-corruption-related issues.

Based on the analysis of the different pilot programs' outcomes and stakeholders' surveys in a variety of programs, the following are the major recommendations from the Polish experience for the effective mainstreaming of anti-corruption contents in the business education curriculum:

- Ensure sufficient faculty-level resources through training and development. This capacity building needs to be sufficient for the level and degree of the proposed integration.

- Cultivate academic integrity as the sine qua non of responsible management education through the discovery, articulation, and institutionalization of the core values of academic ethos in daily academic activities.

- Promote context-specific content development by linking anti-corruption with core management topics.

- Motivate regulatory bodies, accreditation agencies, and corporations to actively participate in program design and delivery. Create opportunities to promote and facilitate anti-corruption and integrity research by faculty members and students for inclusion in future curricula.

- Develop practice-oriented teaching materials that add relevance and realism to classroom activities in order to prepare students for managing corruption and other integrity problems in business and related professions.

2.4 Experience from Germany

The Goethe Business School at the University of Frankfurt in Germany used the Anti-Corruption Toolkit for its business ethics course in the specialized Master in Finance program. The Goethe Business School covers post-experience programs that largely focus on finance after a shift away from its previous MBA, Executive MBA, and general management focus in the aftermath of the financial crisis. Located in the House of Finance, the school draws on the largest agglomeration of finance experts and faculty members in academia (400+) in Europe. The House of Finance offers state-of-the-art facilities and is based on the brand new EUR 1.4 billion campus in Frankfurt's city center. In the semester-long course on ethics, 40 students benefited from the international variety of examples offered by the Toolkit, including the readings and cases.

The Toolkit was flexibly used locally by choosing core and mandatory readings and suggestions for further reading. Selected case studies and exercises were sourced from this Toolkit. An interesting insight that emerged during the program was that the Toolkit is much richer and deeper than the Chartered Financial Analyst (CFA) qualifications exams actually require. The specialized degree program enabled the participants to prepare well for the CFA qualification by contrasting the more elaborate Toolkit with the more limited preparation material for the CFA tests. The participants' reactions to more thorough preparation were extremely positive. They appreciated having received training that could differentiate them from others taking the CFA test. Further, anti-corruption and compliance are core issues on their employers' and management's radar. The course participants confirmed that they felt well prepared for job interviews, negotiations for promotion, or simply projects they would be running at work.

Hence, faculty looking for a wealth of resources will find helpful content when consulting the Toolkit. During the integration process, it became clear that the Toolkit could be used to create an awareness of normative management concepts with which the participants were not really familiar. Most of the courses preceding the ethics course focused on finance and quantitative skills. It is therefore essential that not only anti-corruption but also ethics or any other normative thoughts do not remain isolated in the program design and delivery. A much more successful approach would, throughout the program and beyond, render the participants sensitive to holistic and sound management from the very beginning.

The Anti-Corruption Toolkit is available online free of charge. Participants can use it for self-paced, self-driven learning about other aspects they have identified as most interesting. This feature can create a positive learning atmosphere that decreases dependence on a professor as the main source of information.

2.5 Ethics and anti-corruption teaching and research: a global social role

Worldwide, university and college anti-corruption and integrity teachers and researchers have an important societal role to play. They have the duty and opportunity to help prepare future professionals and public leaders to practice their professions with integrity and to exercise their leadership without corruption. This mission is especially critical in societies where corruption is rife; where preparedness to deal with corruption and ethical problems can make the difference between new graduates succeeding or failing to preserve their integrity in the working world. In challenging governance environments, university graduates and young professionals who wish to behave ethically and live according to their moral values face a daunting task.

In these contexts, lying, cheating, and stealing have become accepted as a way to get ahead in the professions. Bribery, fraud, and kickbacks are systematically used, and even encouraged, in corporations as a means of doing business. In low-paid government jobs in some countries, pressure is commonly applied by superiors and colleagues to extort money from citizens in exchange for public services or special treatment. Even in the nonprofit or civil-society sector, the competition for resources can drive professionals to use "whatever means possible" to win grants and contracts and to gain public acclaim. Although some executives consider integrity a "personal matter," its practice is often deeply affected by organizational contexts and practices.

When integrating the Anti-Corruption Toolkit and related curricular content into teaching courses around the world, professors and lecturers have three major concerns: (1) ensuring the relevance and realism of the curricular content and its fit with the concepts and approaches in the courses and discipline; (2) a political concern – anti-corruption courses often touch on sensitive political issues and organizational practices (even those within the universities themselves). They must be approved by, or at least be acceptable to, the university authorities and supervising ministries and agencies; (3) the need for knowledge and competence to teach the courses, modules, or classes on anti-corruption and integrity within the framework of the university curriculum and existing courses. These three factors will be dealt with in detail in the sections that follow.

2.5.1 Relevance and realism of curricular content

Teachers at universities and colleges seeking to incorporate courses or content on anti-corruption and integrity must first design their teaching activities to ensure that they refer to the real-life ethical issues faced in workplaces. This kind of course material is especially important in management education and executive programs where participants are adult learners with work-life experience, who seek to learn new skills relevant to their professional lives and careers. With this in mind, courses should introduce ethical values and integrity practices that the participants can apply to reason ethically in real-life situations and deal ethically with the pressures, expectations, and obligations that are commonly experienced in the workplace.

The Toolkit is a publicly accessible asset in the hands of professors and researchers interested in anti-corruption and integrity. It is easily adaptable for local use in multiple disciplines. Its modules' flexibility and versatility enable it to be adjusted to a course's subject matter and time constraints. By focusing on core topics that are essential for global discussions, it presents teaching faculty and researchers with concrete examples and practical case studies to liven up class discussions.

In the People's Republic of China, anti-corruption academics strive to design courses that address corruption risks in competitive work environments, where the use of bribes is common and abuse of authority is expected in organizations without effective governance systems. One such professor from Tsinghua University in Beijing uses cases in the news to highlight the moral hazards. Case teaching helps his students deal with the ethical dilemmas of having to make moral compromises to achieve the expected results, or just to keep a job. In some challenging circumstances, pressures from corrupt supervisors and colleagues may force a professional to take part in a malfeasance conspiracy or to cover up a wrongdoing. Scenarios from actual cases of corruption also highlight the legal risks and moral consequences of engaging in malpractices in order to fit in with a work group.

2.5.2 Approval and support of the authorizing environment

The business of university teaching and executive education is conducted in the contexts of institutions with hierarchies of oversight and supervision. Anti-corruption courses sometimes have to deal with issues related to integrity challenges in domestic politics, university practices, and in society at large. The discourses and anti-corruption research may be perceived as challenging the authority of university overseers and political masters. For instance, university administrators in China consider the anti-corruption subject area highly sensitive; the content of these courses are closely monitored. Some administrators perceive these courses as being critical of or subversive to the practices of the Chinese government and business elites and regard them with suspicion. Where teaching and research are deemed to erode the legitimacy of authority and tarnish the reputation of institutions and individuals, scholars may expect a backlash.

During a conference on integrity education for Arab scholars in Egypt in 2011 (during the Arab Spring), professors interested in introducing anti-corruption courses were primarily concerned with how university administrations would perceive their new courses or modules, especially those professors who came from autocratic regimes where teachers and writers commenting on official corruption are traditionally not tolerated. Corruption issues remain a common factor in the mass demonstrations and rallying calls for democracy from Tunisia and Libya to Jordan and Egypt. University administrators and public authorities are highly sensitive to any public discourse or discussion on the issue of corruption. While the experiences of Arab scholars during the Arab Spring uprising may be an outlier, professors and researchers from East Asia and the Middle East to Eastern Europe and Central Asia have commented on the need for official authorization and support for them to feel safe to introduce anti-corruption courses and modules.[1]

The Toolkit not only can provide scholars with adaptable and updated curricular content, but its global signature under the PRME initiative of the UN Global Compact also lends legitimacy to the scholars who adopt its content. Scholars and institutions adopting the Toolkit may also select different elements from different topics to specifically address certain issues in a politically acceptable way (e.g., broadly discussing market failures and principal-agent problems, introducing local legislation, and international standards), while staying clear of the most locally sensitive topics.

2.5.3 Faculty expertise and motivation

Faculty expertise and motivation are critical for a successful and sustainable introduction of courses, modules, or classes on anti-corruption and integrity within the framework of university courses and executive programs. This is where the Anti-Corruption Toolkit can have a tremendous impact in facilitating anti-corruption education. The Toolkit presents topical areas of knowledge (including foundational concepts and key disciplinary theories) with study questions, an extensive bibliography,

---

1 Interviews with professors and researchers in the Public Integrity Education Network in Indonesia, China, Armenia, Lebanon, Egypt, Israel, and Bulgaria.

literature and reading materials, case studies, study questions, and teacher resources. These resources offer teachers and researchers a wide smorgasbord of curricular materials that have been nominated and reviewed by an international group of peers with a substantial background in teaching and researching anti-corruption. With this globally sourced cache of peer-reviewed materials, teachers can put together the basic materials for teaching a curriculum and a research agenda.

There are very few semester-long courses on anti-corruption or integrity offered at universities around the world and models of such curricula are rare. For example, in China, there were about 400 academics and researchers writing and publishing on the subject of anti-corruption in 2011, and they were from some 45 universities, colleges, and research centers. However, only seven universities were known to offer semester-length courses on anti-corruption and integrity. In addition, new courses on anti-corruption often have to compete with existing courses for time slots in fully packed curricula; introducing them requires teachers to integrate the new materials in existing courses and activities. When using the Toolkit, case studies and teaching materials from around the world will not only provide teachers with ready-to-use and easily adaptable content, they will also provide students with interesting cases for class discussion and exercises. With access to these online and regularly updated resources, implementing modern anti-corruption curricula locally should become much easier.

2.6 Conclusions

Teachers of management may be the only people standing between the cohorts of students, who come to learn the skills of their management profession, and their future work lives ridden with temptations to engage in corrupt practices. Universities and colleges often overlook the need to prepare their graduates to safeguard their integrity in challenging ethical situations and corrupting work environments after their graduation. When business schools teach only idealized textbook models and theoretical constructs on how the business world works, they often omit the real-life challenges; they may omit the thorny ethical issues faced by management professionals, such as cut-throat tactics and competitive strategies involving the use of bribery and fraud. Students of management, especially those in executive programs, come to learn the skills and knowledge of the profession, not only as they should be, but also as they are practiced in real life. This orientation will help adequately prepare future generations of managers in various industries for challenging careers ahead. Invariably, graduates from executive programs and university courses in corruption-prone societies and industries will have to contend with corruption and other moral issues in their professions and daily lives. Hence, management schools must consider offering courses and curricular content on anti-corruption and integrity to better prepare students for the real world of work.

To meet this pressing need for ethical competence, the Anti-Corruption Toolkit presents an open source, easily accessible, and regularly updated library of curricular materials for teachers and researchers. Its materials have been contributed and reviewed by a network of international scholars interested and skilled in the subject matter. The course contents, case studies, bibliography of references, and study exercises can be adapted to courses in various contexts and of different durations.

We are all responsible for creating a moral frame for the legal and ethical behavior of organizational members and the organization:

1. Through extensive ethical education of business people and, more broadly, people in all professions, using behavioral models, case studies, critical analysis, and skill sets such as Socratic thinking, which can illuminate the issues of corruption;

2. By improving public sector ethics, the development of a robust culture of institutional governance, and the introduction of anti-corruption legislation, all of which are necessary parts of a unified regime of anti-corruption based on law, as well as on institutional and administrative arrangements (McKoy, 2010);

3. Through formal systems designed to prevent unethical and illegal behavior – systems including senior executive oversight, codes of conduct, communication and training programs, anonymous reporting systems, and clear disciplinary measures for misconduct, especially by taking the following practical steps:

   - Drafting anti-corruption principles within the ethical code of conduct that can be applied in all countries in which a company operates

   - Encouraging departments to encourage their suppliers to promote the application of anti-corruption policies in order to maintain the image and integrity of both parties

- Prohibiting employees from making political contributions on behalf of the company, or using the company's name, funds, property, or equipment for the support of political parties

- Explicitly stating that employees are not allowed to accept gifts, gratuities, or kickbacks – also identified as the return of a percentage of a sum of money already received, typically as a result of pressure, coercion, or a secret agreement – which are usually offered in an attempt to win contracts or influence decision outcomes

- Making explicit that, where friends and family have an interest, personal influence must not play a role in securing business for the company

- Putting in place audit committees that not only allow employees to raise concerns about accounting and auditing matters, but also to enable them to flag unethical behavior such as bribery or corruption

- Running ethical training programs in order to create awareness among employees, to convince them to resist any temptation and crackdown on corruption

- Creating a series of case study situations or simulations in which employees are faced with bribery and corruption challenges, and encouraging discussions and comments that help them understand the issues faced in the real world

- Linking performance management to ethical behavior, and adherence to explicitly propagated ethical principles; using performance appraisal as an opportunity to discipline those who engage in off-shore business illegalities

- Creating and supporting international anti-corruption initiatives

Yet there is a limit to what can be taught. As Alexander Solzhenitsyn wrote, "even the most rational approach to ethics is defenseless if there is not the will to do what is right."

Reference

McKoy, D.V. (2009). Defining corruption. In A. Stachowicz-Stanusch (Ed.). *Organizational Immunity to Corruption: Building Theoretical and Research Foundations*. Warsaw: Polish Academy of Sciences.

3
Linking the anti-corruption curriculum to pedagogy
Selecting teaching methods in context

Chapter 2 discussed how the Anti-Corruption Toolkit offers a wider range of choices for course design that takes into account the need for customization in developing learning goals and content. In practice, pedagogy needs to be aligned with the chosen content and desired learning outcomes. This chapter shows how an effective link between content design and pedagogical methods can be used to enhance curriculum impact.

Choices regarding learning outcomes and content are key elements in developing a good management curriculum. This process is influenced by a number of context-specific factors, such as target-audience characteristics and desired course outcomes to achieve objectives of improving knowledge and skill. In developing a course to target company executives with the aim of helping them to make difficult business decisions with due consideration of ethics and integrity issues, faculty needs to understand that business decisions are often context specific. For example, a decision regarding employment creation versus short-term profitability could create a trade-off dilemma. As businesses become increasingly dynamic, work environments are becoming more unstable, which could easily foster economic crime (PricewaterhouseCoopers, 2009).

In addition to the target audience, which is scrutinized in the needs analysis, a wider moral responsibility of higher education institutions and the business school is to create the need to deliver integrity and therefore to develop capacity to learn and absorb relevant information. The needs-analysis or context-specific view may lead to a transactional curriculum for selling the concept but may be far from facilitating the spirit of universalism in ethical conduct, which is one of the fundamental objectives of the Toolkit.

Bribery and corruption are prime examples of undesirable behavior. They have become critical concerns for governments as well as companies in many developed and developing countries. In these environments, education can be a powerful factor in anti-corruption efforts (Beets, 2005; Charlesworth, 2008). In addition to teaching and research, active business school intervention can place the educational institution's advocacy role at the core of stakeholder linkages. Consensus among today's university students that bribery and corruption are harmful will influence the future ethical climate of businesses (Grünbaum, 1997; Jaffe and Tsimerman, 2005). As future specialists, executives, or entrepreneurs, today's students are of critical importance in resisting corrupt practices because they will influence business activities once they gain decision-making authority.

Taking these considerations into account, this chapter explores these questions:

- What are the common anti-corruption curriculum objectives for different contexts?

- How can Toolkit components be combined for maximum effectiveness?

- How can the institution's culture influence Toolkit development and implementation?

- How can individual pedagogical methods best respond to the institution's distinctive cultural requirements?

This chapter offers a framework that will help to identify anti-corruption curriculum objectives, select content, and use pedagogical methods for maximum effectiveness. In view of the possibility of stand-alone, adapted, or hybrid curricula, an effort has been made to offer a generic syllabus that includes a survey of related subject matter.

3.1 Curriculum objectives

The omnipresence of corruption has generated several international initiatives that are intended to promote the inclusion of anti-corruption-related subjects in management education curricula at universities and business schools. As the issues related to corruption cannot be generalized, any educational initiative must focus on emphasizing the relevance to the context. At the same time, we need to look at universally acceptable responses to deal with the analysis of the problem. While this balancing remains a major overall goal of the curriculum, the decision on specific learning outcomes shapes the direction and scope of the curriculum.

The learning outcomes of anti-corruption curriculum development are linked to the learning objectives in a given context. While learning objectives will vary in different contexts, specific knowledge–skill goals could be selected using the available framework for the purpose. Bloom's Taxonomy (Bloom *et al.*, 1956) suggests these learning goals: knowledge, comprehension, application, analysis, synthesis, and evaluation. Krathwohl (2002) suggested a modified version of Bloom's Taxonomy by focusing on two dimensions at a time.

The first knowledge dimension includes different types of knowledge: factual, conceptual, procedural, and metacognitive. The second cognitive process dimension includes the following: remember, understand, apply, analyze, evaluate, and create. While applying the framework to the context of the Anti-Corruption Toolkit, the knowledge and cognitive process dimensions can be established. Tripathi *et al.* (2014) attempted to apply the taxonomy to education about poverty and sustainability issues in management. While mapping the learning objectives for the proposed Toolkit curriculum, the learning objectives can be identified by applying the modified Bloom's Taxonomy (Krathwohl, 2002). The conceptualized framework is presented in Table 3.1.

Knowledge dimensions	Cognitive process dimension					
	Remember	**Understand**	**Apply**	**Analyze**	**Evaluate**	**Create**
Facts about corruption in the context	Objective$_1$					
Conceptual issues in developing knowledge framework			Objective$_2$			
Procedural issues in addressing corruption						
Strategic knowledge of the situation and possible solutions				Objective$_3$		Objective$_n$

TABLE 3.1 Applying Bloom and Krathwohl's framework to define learning objectives

The framework in Table 3.1 is a proposed learning-objective mapping tool for the desired anti-corruption curriculum. If the course is not stand-alone, the objectives may be merged with the other existing objectives. It is important to note that the objectives can be identified by combining and analyzing both of the dimensions in the framework, i.e., corruption-related and integrity-related knowledge, and the specific cognitive skills set.

3.2 Cultural context

Anti-corruption is a global issue and, to be effective, teaching needs to be done on a global scale. For example, Watkins (2000) highlights that in order to incorporate concepts from one country in course material devised for another, the overall context of the society has to be examined. As the most recent paradigm in educational research, situated learning theory says learning cannot be separated from the context in which it occurs (Alexander *et al.* 2009). Hence, the culture-learning style connection has to be applied if anti-corruption education is to be implemented internationally. The cultural orientation affects the learning style of the target group. Hofstede's (1991) social-value typology helps to understand cultures in terms of different dimensions: power distance, individualism vs. collectivism, masculinity vs. femininity, uncertainty avoidance, and long-term vs. short-term orientation.

On the basis of these dimensions, one can define the culture as "high-context" or "low-context," and the context has direct implications for the selection of learning methods. The following example of an incident relating to Toolkit integration shows how power distance can influence the target group's preferred learning style.

In a recent faculty development workshop in an Asian country with relatively high power distance in terms of Hofstede's framework, the learning style of the adult and mature target group of faculty was found to be focused and teacher-centric. During the workshop, the group members were given open-ended analytical questions to build capacity around thinking and analyzing. They did not participate as well as expected. They wanted to assume minimal roles and expected the sessions to be teacher-centric, with a focus on faculty delivery.

Research has shown that students differ in their learning approaches, depending on their cultural socialization (Joy and Kolb 2009). In order to make a strong impact on student awareness and their attitude and behavior toward corruption, it can be assumed that different learning approaches have to be taken into account. Based on his experiential learning cycle, Kolb (1984) defines four learning styles. Whereas the cycles of (1) concrete experience, (2) reflective observation, (3) abstract conceptualization, and (4) active experimentation are assumed to be universal, the preferences for individual learning styles (diverging, assimilating, converging, and accommodating) depend heavily on cultural socialization.

The four phases of the learning cycle can be activated by different learning methods and techniques:

- **Concrete experience (1)** – present own experiences of corruption or an authentic case of corruption

- **Reflective observation (2)** – analyze experiences via group discussion

- **Abstract conceptualization (3)** – understand experiences with scientific theories and models via listening to experts, or reading their papers

- **Active experimentation** (4) – apply existing knowledge in authentic situations via simulations, role plays, or case studies in order to create new concrete experiences

The experiences of some pilot schools can be linked to Kolb's learning cycle. These schools observed that local culture influences how students learn and therefore developed solutions to prepare lecture material and other pedagogical tools. The following example of a Polish pilot school shows how concrete experience on the one hand and cultural context on the other can play a role in introducing the corruption theme to students.

A Polish pilot school (see also Chapter 2) described case analysis, especially of short cases, as a helpful method to recognize various aspects of corruption and ethical dilemmas from different points of view. Because of the lack of regional case studies, the method was adapted to a Polish cultural context, as students were asked to write live cases in groups in their mother tongue. The cases focused on widely commented on and interesting corruption scandals in Poland over the last decade. The case study structure included the course of events connected with the situation, the causes of corruption that were revealed, actions taken against corruption, social response, legal consequences and other sanctions, and corruption consequences. The project resulted in well-developed case studies of Polish corruption scandals that may be used in future discussions during lectures on anti-corruption behavior. In some of the case content not only the scandals were described, but also effective corruption prevention steps in the Polish context.

In the active experimentation phase and to involve students in anti-corruption issues outside the classroom, students were asked to work in groups and prepare visual material or a movie that would popularize anti-corruption attitudes and could be associated with their presented case. Students prepared T-shirts, cups, posters, and short films that were also presented and discussed by their colleagues.

To achieve reflective student observation, the lecturer needs to handle the course as a discussion leader and fellow colleague, not as an infallible instructor or an authority who cannot be challenged. Different or dissenting views should be welcomed with tolerance and openness. The lecturer must welcome questions and suggestions in actual and virtual discussions.[1]

Situated learning theory teaching has to be adapted to culture and learning styles in order to strengthen the influence of teaching on anti-corruption awareness, attitude, and behavior. For example, a Russian pilot school assumed that every MBA student had encountered at least a few manifestations of corruption in his/her professional life. Students declared that they personally understood that corruption is a bad thing. At the same time, most students said that corruption in Russia did not constitute deviant behavior, but rather the opposite! Many students spoke of "coercion to corruption" from outside the company as a major problem. The pilot school also observed that by talking about corruption in a group discussion, students got excited and did not remain silent and indifferent. They intuitively understood that corruption is dangerous. Questions such as how and why corruption is dangerous were discussed. But in Russia there is a common belief that corruption is inevitable, and that it does not depend on a single person's decision. An attempt to talk about the manifestations of corruption from personal experience brought the discussion to a deadlock. The students began to complain of despair, asking "What can I do

1 See syllabus in the Appendix.

alone against the system?" This sense of danger and despair led to a student group's rejection of the need to include the anti-corruption course in the MBA curriculum:

> We do not need this course. In general, corruption is a big issue, it is harmful to the business, and it is dangerous to a manager. But we cannot correct the environment by discussing it in a classroom. Tomorrow, we will have to operate our businesses in circumstances where all these ethical ideas are not applicable. We are just wasting our time.

The Russian pilot school concluded that students will initially respond negatively to the introduction of an anti-corruption course in the MBA curriculum, as they do not see the immediate practical value. It is therefore very important to design the first introductory session correctly. It is necessary to motivate students to study the course. This motivation depends on the national context. The pilot school mentioned that in Russia, for example, the additional external stimulus can be used that, in the near future, there will be a requirement for an anti-corruption compliance function in every company, even if it is a medium or a small business. Second, since the issue of corruption is perceived to be acute and personal, it is suggested that a lecturer does not start the course with a discussion based on the personal experiences of the students. One should also not start the course with general concepts that might be seen as a moralizing form of education. The best suggestion is to start with an existing problem presented through a case study that has a positive solution.

Based on the theoretical frameworks and experiences drawn from the different piloting cultural contexts, we may establish that the analysis of the cultural context is significant in enhancing the impact of the curriculum in the given context. This will also help to align the curriculum objectives and select the pedagogy to suit the learning characteristics of the target learning groups.

3.3 Packaging the anti-corruption course syllabus

The PRME Anti-Corruption Toolkit addresses the following topics related to corruption in ten thematic modules:[2]

1. **Fundamental concepts.** The recognition and framing of ethical dilemmas and social responsibility, and their importance in strategic decision making

2. **Economics, market failure, and professional dilemmas**

3. **Legislation, control by law, agency, and fiduciary duty**

4. **Why corruption?** Findings of behavioral science

5. **Gifts, side deals, and conflicts of interest.** Legislation and cases to understand gifts, side deals, and conflicts of interest as well as the lies and obfuscation that are often used to conceal them

6. **International standards and supply chain issues.** Frameworks and analytic methods for discussing the problems that companies face and the need to be aware of moral standards across borders, and local customs such as bribery

7. **Managing anti-corruption issues.** Designing, implementing, and overseeing corporate ethics and

2 actoolkit.unprme.org.

compliance systems in response to local and global compliance regimes

8. **Functional department and collective action roles in combating corruption.** The functional departments examined include human resources, marketing, accounting, and finance

9. **Truth and disclosure, whistleblowing, and loyalty.** These topics raise issues of timing and context regarding circumstances in which it is permissible for an agent or employee to blow the whistle on corruption

10. **The developing global anti-corruption compliance regime.** Topics include (a) global public policy principles and how they are enforced (e.g., UN Global Compact's Tenth Principle and the UN Convention against Corruption; OECD Anti-Corruption Principles); and (b) links between corruption and forms of state failure, such as deprivation of human rights and environmental degradation

The Toolkit curriculum is designed to be flexible, and the modules may be taught individually or together as part of a freestanding course on anti-corruption. The curriculum serves as a guideline set out for faculty and prescribes what needs to be taught on anti-corruption-related subjects in management education. It also outlines methods to ensure that each student has learned the necessary material. Faculty members can select elements from the Toolkit consisting of (a) core concept readings, (b) case studies, (c) primary source documents, and (d) study questions or scenarios for class discussion, and integrate them into their own courses. In a crossover section of the Toolkit,

(e) teaching method suggestions can be utilized in a variety of different cultural environments and classroom settings. The ten modules of the management education curriculum provide faculty with these resources. Each module contains the different components: rationale, learning methods, study questions, core literature, and additional literature. The organization of the Toolkit is represented in Figure 3.1.

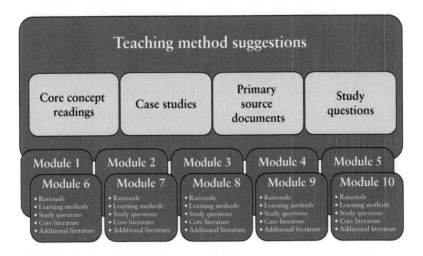

FIGURE 3.1   PRME model curriculum

Whether it is a complete stand-alone ethics, integrity, and anti-corruption-focused syllabus or a few lectures that integrate anti-corruption in a conventional management course, the Toolkit can be used effectively. At this point, we can also briefly look into the differences between a curriculum and a syllabus. In contrast to a curriculum, a syllabus is typically composed by each individual lecturer and focuses on a particular class. It usually offers an overview of the goals of the course so that students know what is expected of them by the end of the term.

The following example of a course syllabus, "Corruption development and democracy: Theories, policies, and best practices,"[3] may serve as a model. The aims of this course are to expose students to relevant theories and analyses of the impact of corruption and its interactions with development and democracy. It also discusses the range and results of various governance and anti-corruption policies and strategies that have been tried in several countries. Finally, the course will analyze the practices of accountability and anti-corruption organizations in select jurisdictions. By the end of the course, students will have a strong foundation for understanding the sources of corruption and be enabled to develop and implement approaches that work in different contexts. As a learning method, case studies of effective and ineffective accountability and anti-corruption organizations will be used. In order to achieve the course objectives, the model course is conceptualized and presented in Table 3.2. The purpose is to demonstrate how the syllabus contents linked to the context-specific issues can be packaged as a course module, irrespective of the relative credit and positioning in the overall degree program.

---

3 Syllabus is kindly provided by Professor Bolongaita, Carnegie Mellon Heinz College.

	Session 1
Topic	Introduction: Corruption, development, and democracy
	Session 2
Topic	Corruption: An overview
Readings	Michael Johnston, *Syndromes of corruption,* chapters 1-2. Robert Klitgaard, "A holistic approach to fighting corruption," 2008 Vito Tanzi, "Corruption around the world: Causes, consequences, scope and cures," International Monetary Fund, 1998
Study questions	What is corruption? What are its causes? What are its consequences?
	Session 3
Topic	Corruption: Types and trends
Readings Primary sources	Michael Johnston, Syndromes of corruption, chapter 3. *Case Study: China* Yan Sun, "Corruption, growth and reform: The Chinese enigma," *Current History*, September 2005 "Corruption: No ordinary Zhou," *The Economist*, 2 August 2014 "Corruption and the economy," *The Economist*, 2 August 2014
Study questions	What are the different types/kinds of corruption? Why is corruption in China an enigma?
	Session 4
Topic	Corruption: Perceptions versus reality
Readings Primary sources	Transparency International, Corruption Perceptions Index 2013, Transparency International, Bribe Payers Index 2011, Transparency International, Global Corruption Barometer 2013, all at www.transparency.org *Case study: Australia* Organization for Economic Cooperation and Development, *Report on implementing the OECD Convention on Bribery in Australia* ABC News, "Australia 'failing' to tackle bribery by multinational companies: OECD"
Study questions	…

TABLE 3.2 Example syllabus

One of the most useful aspects of a syllabus is that it frequently gives students an idea of the course schedule, listing the dates and descriptions of assignments and tests. For these aspects, please see the complete syllabus in the Appendix of this book.

3.4 Aligning objectives, contents, and pedagogy in the context: a framework

After the Toolkit launched in 2014, members of the PRME Working Group on Anti-Corruption and pilot schools[4] were asked to share their experiences with syllabi created with the help of the Toolkit. As an overall framework, the Toolkit was considered to be an effective and valuable source of material. Many of the pilot schools highlighted some of the material provided as useful for teaching because it sheds light on mechanisms of dealing with corruption.

Apart from this strength, the multidisciplinary nature of the Toolkit may inspire local faculty to create new courses. Multiplicity can also be perceived as a weakness. Some of the evaluating pilot schools mentioned the lack of regional or local examples, so lecturers should search for material that fits the local context and customize material and methodologies for specific context needs. The thematic modules that have been the most frequently used corruption topics in pilot schools are (1) Fundamental concepts, (6) International standards and supply chain issues, and (10) The developing global anti-corruption compliance regime. To summarize, pilot schools say Toolkit integration is challenging. All of them selected parts of the Toolkit, rather than trying to offer all the topics in a single course. In some cases, creating one or two sessions to parachute into existing courses seems to be the best way to introduce corruption-related topics.

One of the pilot schools offered a course on governance and ethics that presented business ethics and corporate governance concepts and showed how these concepts are critical for 21st-century business success. One session explored the components of an

---

4 Pilot schools are located in Argentina, France, India, Nigeria, Poland, Russia, Tanzania, Ukraine, South Africa, and Switzerland.

effective ethics management program. The focus was on the role of a code of ethics, with specific attention to gifts, insider trading, and conflict of interest. The lecturer used parts of the modules (5) Gifts, side deals, and conflicts of interest, and (9) Truth and disclosure, whistleblowing, and loyalty, to prepare the session.

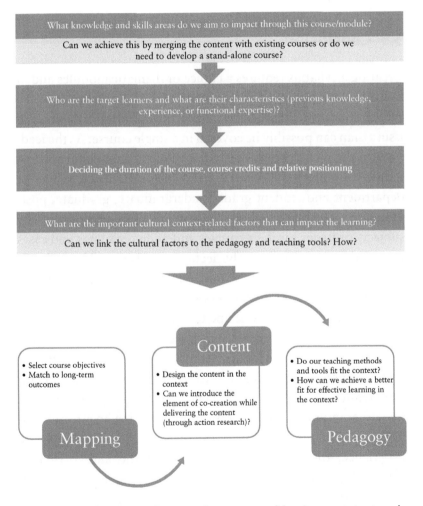

FIGURE 3.2   Aligning anti-corruption course objectives, content and pedagogy in the context

These pilot school experiences and the impact of context-related learning objectives suggest a detailed step-by-step process framework to develop an effective anti-corruption-related course with a focus on the different issues that were discussed earlier in this chapter (Figure 3.2).

3.5 Conclusion

Creating a syllabus requires a choice of thematic modules and of individual readings and assignments based on the topics in the PRME model curriculum because it covers more subjects and issues than can possibly be covered in a single course. As the feedback of the pilot schools showed, it requires choices for sectors, industries, countries, and issues, and customization to school or department and student grade (undergraduate, graduate, postgraduate). Most pilot schools undertook a pre-selection of key subjects or issues for their courses and added readings and cases provided in the Toolkit. The lecturer is also confronted with contextual choices and learning styles. Not all methodologies will work in all settings. Success stories (e.g., Poland) and failures (e.g., Russia) help to shape the syllabus, as well as student feedback about their interests and necessities. In summary, the attempt to impose a uniform syllabus on a multicultural student body requires careful attention to student sensibilities and cultural reality. The cultural context and learning objectives are the two other important considerations in designing an effective syllabus. Based on the analysis of the theories and context-specific experience, the proposed framework for the anti-corruption course alignment may help to realize a high-impact course with adequate balance among the objectives, contents, and pedagogy.

References

Alexander, P.A., Schallert, D.L., & Reynolds, R.E. (2009). What is learning anyway? A topographical perspective considered. *Educational Psychologist*, 44(3), pp. 176-192.

Beets, S. (2005). Understanding the demand-side issues of international corruption. *Journal of Business Ethics*, 57(1), pp. 65-81.

Bloom, B.S., Engelhart, M.D., Furst, E.J., Hill, W.H., & Krathwohl, D.R. (1956). *Taxonomy of Educational Objectives: The Classification of Educational Goals. Handbook I: Cognitive Domain.* New York: David McKay.

Charlesworth, Z. (2008). Learning styles across cultures: Suggestions for educators. *Education and Training*, 50(2), pp. 115-127.

Grünbaum, L. (1997). Attitudes of future managers towards business ethics: A comparison of Finnish and American business students. *Journal of Business Ethics*, 16(4), pp. 451-463.

Hofstede, G. (1991). *Cultures and Organizations: Software of the Mind.* New York: McGraw-Hill.

Jaffe, E.D., & Tsimerman, A. (2005). Business ethics in a transition economy: Will the next Russian generation be any better? *Journal of Business Ethics*, 62(1), pp. 87-97.

Joy, S., & Kolb, D.A. (2009). Are there cultural differences in learning style? *International Journal of Intercultural Relations*, 33, pp. 69-85.

Kolb, D.A. (1984). *Experiential Learning.* Upper Saddle River, NJ: Prentice Hall.

Krathwohl, D.R. (2002). A Revision of Bloom's Taxonomy: An Overview. *Theory Into Practice*, 41 (4), pp. 212-218.

PricewaterhouseCoopers (2009). *Economic Crime in a Downturn: The 5th Global Economic Crime Survey.* London: Author.

Tripathi, S., Prakash, A., & Amann, W. (2014). Management education with poverty alleviation focus: A framework for curriculum design and pedagogical alignment packaging the course. Presentation of a proposed book chapter at Responsible Management Education Research Conference at HTW, Chur, Switzerland, on October 31.

Watkins, D. (2000). Learning and teaching: A cross-cultural perspective. *School Leadership and Management*, 20(2), pp. 161-173.

4
Anti-Corruption Toolkit

Adaptations to the specific context of executive education

From the very beginning of the recent financial crisis in 2007, executive education expenses were the first to be cut in many companies. But executive education is now moving forward again: cutting executive education was not a prudent response to the financial crisis. Education is critical to address problems that require fresh views, new skills, and motivated executives.

In this more challenging business environment, companies were at risk of senior executives and managers using ethics creatively to achieve business or financial objectives. In many countries, such as the People's Republic of China, corruption has soared, despite an increase in available knowledge on how to prevent it and government initiatives to fight it (e.g., see Gibbs, 2014). This implies that mere education will not be effective in realizing anti-corruption goals unless it has been effectively linked to sound behavior modification interventions through pedagogy.

Although many countries and companies still feel the effects of the financial crisis, executive education budgets have normalized somewhat (Amann *et al.*, 2014, Introduction). This positive development offers an opportunity for business schools to develop effective anti-corruption teaching materials for use in executive education seminars. This opportunity will enable them to better fulfill their social responsibilities and to function as agents of positive change.

If the faculty is on board, executive education seminars can be easier to run than degree programs, which typically take place over a longer timeframe. This chapter, with its particular focus on executive education seminars, details four crucial challenges and four solutions, and lays out how to contribute to improved company resistance to corrupt practices.

4.1 Core executive education adaptation challenges

We encountered four challenges in our efforts to launch, implement, and evaluate executive education programs. These experiences and anecdotal evidence are summarized below.

4.1.1 Different tasks at the executive education level

Unlike executive education programs, graduate and undergraduate curricula focus on teaching knowledge and developing skills. Comparison between the two approaches relates to the distinction between **red ocean** business acumen seminars and **blue ocean** seminars that emphasize collaborative problem solving.

Red ocean seminars include general workshops on strategy, leadership, international management, marketing, and ethics and compliance topics. There is an abundance of such standardized, bread-and-butter seminars, as well as potential faculties and institutions to offer them. Business schools have recognized that there is limited scope to differentiate, at least on the content side, in these segments. Instead, the best business schools add value by building up student skills to co-create solutions to problems.

When the Anti-Corruption Toolkit is applied to executive education seminars, it is essential to understand such a program's distinct needs to focus on the co-creation of answers to respond to current or future challenges and to adapt its content and learning exercises to the program participants' particular situations. Exercises that require reading the latest articles on local challenges, or compiling their own short and concise cases, need to be integrated into the scope of executive education seminars. The Anti-Corruption Toolkit provides material that can be used for most if not all of the undergraduate and graduate curriculum, but executive education needs to be co-creative in concept and design.

4.1.2 Program participants as products instead of customers

Business undergraduate or graduate degree candidates understand – and perhaps even expect – that the learning process entails massive changes in their knowledge and skills levels. Typically, they are younger and more malleable than the senior white-collar individuals in executive education seminars. Having achieved much in their lives and possessing more on-the-job experience, executive education participants expect a high degree of customization. In fact, the human resources departments that award contracts to business schools are likely to demand it on behalf of employee-consumers.

While business schools seek to "rewire brains," "install new mental software," and alter behaviors in fundamental ways, executive education has the task of enabling participants to question basic assumptions, thereby transforming them from customers into products. Ensuring participants are both customers and products is also linked to the next point, which concerns time horizons.

4.1.3 Different time horizons

Undergraduate programs can be multiyear in length. Master's programs are shorter, but still cover a long period. In contrast to the two-year MBA tradition in the United States, Europe tends to have more one-year programs. Some schools – such as INSEAD's MBA – allow schools, program directors, and faculty members to work with participants for at least ten months.

In contrast, executive education programs often use one or two modules; each consisting of four days and linked by an action learning project, which covers a maximum of ten months. Face-to-face time is very limited. Some companies and organizations demand that their learning partners and business schools even offer half-day seminars for the most senior executives and treat them as a priority, because they cannot spend much time away from work. To take advantage of the best that different top schools have to offer, other schools with little or no integration across models might provide these half-day seminars, an approach that runs counter to holistic learning models.

Figure 4.1 illustrates two different but not necessarily mutually exclusive learning models. In fact, optimally, they complement one another. The first model differentiates between the emotional stages of the learning experience, and the second illustrates the concrete building blocks needed to achieve these transitions. In the case of anti-corruption education and training, simply asking participants to identify high-risk corruption situations does not teach practitioners how to avoid or detect them.

Executive education lacks a university course's abundant faculty–student interaction points over an extended time. Opportunities to discuss corruption must be seized, because normatively sound management standards are not a recurring topic.

Executive education
learning model 1

Executive education
learning model 2

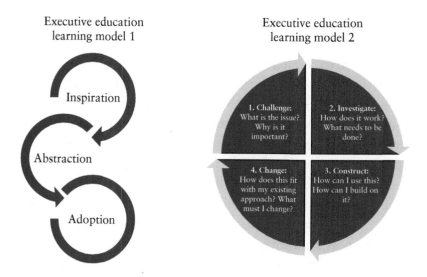

FIGURE 4.1   Overview of key learning models in executive education

As noted earlier, the two models in Figure 4.1 illustrate the three emotional stages of learning and the building blocks needed to achieve an effective transition the next phase (see Amann *et al.*, 2014, Introduction; Strebel and Keys, 2005). It distinguishes between four separate yet equally important tasks to be carried out in order to create high-impact learning.

First, there is a need to challenge established assumptions and establish the topic's relevance and importance. Because corruption is not a specific functional department (e.g., marketing) or a universally more or less identical and shared issue (e.g., economic conditions), devising anti-corruption curricula confronts teachers with unique challenges. All course participants need to understand why the field is so important *to them*, and which specific aspect they need to better understand so that they can become more effective.

For instance, there are many different definitions of corruption (see Chapter 1). What is clearly illegal and unethical in an increasing number of countries may still be normal practice in another country. It takes time to educate course participants about corruption and to outline why selected practices are risky.

The next phase in this learning model looks at investigation. Participants explore the different corporate function types and elements of successful business that might be affected. This is where the richness of the corruption and anti-corruption phenomena deserves space and time, both in degree and executive education programs – with the difference that the latter are usually much more limited in terms of time.

Third, this learning model foresees a phase of active experimentation where the participant works through experience-based corruption scenarios. Again, a thorough exercise, simulation, or in-depth case study, along with a reasonably substantiated, interactive debriefing, takes time.

Fourth, a reflection phase on what it all means for oneself, one's team, and one's organization is also critical because it lays the foundation for change in companies, teams, and executive behavior. In sum, in executive education effective anti-corruption learning interventions may confront the serious time constraints of executive education programs.

4.1.4 Limited market size of anti-corruption courses

Anti-corruption training is most often sought by international companies whose managers have the challenging tasks of bridging two cultures as well as the varying understandings of what normatively sound business conduct is. In reality, however, very few companies specifically request ethics, sustainability, or anti-corruption training. They generally source executive development programs with the help of their requests for proposals, which are phrased much more positively, hardly shedding light on normative management aspects. Because few companies are willing to implicitly or explicitly admit to ethical or corruption concerns, the market for anti-corruption courses is smaller than what business realities might require.

While business schools often pride themselves on ethics and social responsibility core and elective courses, few allow corruption to be the sole or primary focus of interest. As a consequence, few human resources or executive development directors voluntarily add corruption to the list of topics to be dealt with in executive education seminars. Perhaps they fear that internal clients might interpret such a move as an indication that there is a need for it. Where and if anti-corruption seminars are not actively demanded by their client base, few business schools would diversify their current offerings to include anti-corruption topics.

4.2 Solutions

Business schools need to devise an effective response to address these four challenges. The following four approaches have worked in various different cultural and legal environments. They can inspire schools to create their own solutions on site, and can enable faculty and program directors to seize every executive education opportunity.

4.2.1 Positive semantics, labeling, and branding

Business schools can use positive language to start discussions among various stakeholders. Several successful executive education providers have positioned anti-corruption as a critical skills category. We have observed executive education course participants as well as those in sales meetings between business schools and companies or organizations suddenly paying more attention, listening, and becoming more interested in normatively sound management and anti-corruption as topics when they are referred to as **"heart" skills**. They say that the ability to get business done effectively and efficiently without relying on any corruption is critical because business needs to positively affect stakeholders in all settings.

Heart skills require leaders and managers to have a positive impact on individuals with whom they interact or who experience the consequences of our business behavior. The more professional executive education seminars foster heart skills; this will benefit all stakeholders. Few course participants would reject the necessity of heart skills. Faculties could speak about anti-corruption as an essential tool for the next generation of corporate leaders.

4.2.2 Non-negotiable core part of leadership development programs

Anti-corruption training is part of larger leadership and management development objectives that should be non-negotiable in core content. This is where executive education providers need to go beyond being customer-driven and actually *drive* their customers. This book also suggests looking into the blind spots that requests for proposals might have and driving corporate clients and individuals to normative topics – especially anti-corruption (see Amann *et al.*, forthcoming). This approach leads to measures for value-added executive education. The need for anti-corruption to be a non-negotiable core of comprehensive (however short) executive programs will clarify the responsibilities for the sales staff of executive education seminars and for mixed teams that include the faculty. As a result, we suggest adding a sixth layer to the traditional way of measuring executive education's success, going beyond the fairly established but limited approaches suggested by Phillips (2003) and Kirkpatrick (1998 cited in Phillips 2003) (see Figure 4.2).

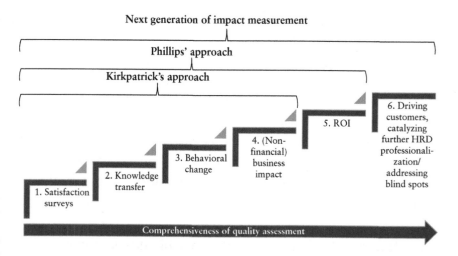

FIGURE 4.2 Measuring the impacts of executive education seminars

4.2.3 Building local and speed capabilities

We also recommend that faculties that offer anti-corruption training consider whether or not to add local, up-to-date, fresh insights. Specific regions might have their own particularities and ways in which corruption and anti-corruption work.

In the Introduction, we referred to corruption and anti-corruption as anti-fragile phenomena. The better our solutions to fight corruption are – be it with the help of more sophisticated legal frameworks or corporate policies – the more sophisticated emerging corruption might become. Corruption is not a static phenomenon; it lives and evolves. It becomes more subtle, more hidden, more creative, more complex, and ever harder to detect. Similar to bacteria becoming resistant to chemicals, the corruption of the future will adopt new forms. This implies that anti-corruption must also evolve in order to keep up with new forms of corruption and must reflect and fight local innovations in the field of corruption more effectively. It is the duty of involved faculty members to see to what extent the Anti-Corruption Toolkit needs newer insights, readings, and cases, or more local elements.

Deans and research directors need to respond more rapidly to developments in the fields of corruption and anti-corruption within their schools and organizations. In effect, anti-corruption education requires "a rapid response team." For instance, timely anti-corruption materials may be needed for different academic departments. Schools need organizational flexibility and some reserve budget for key faculty members to be deployed for emerging corruption challenges. Individual faculty members should not be left alone and deprived of the resources to find solutions and benefit from institutional synergies. Moving beyond the individual faculty member and the executive education institution, networking across institutions on the topic of anti-corruption can help with efforts to develop local and fresh insights for anti-corruption programs.

4.2.4 Going forward

Business schools lose a substantial degree of credibility and impact when they do not talk about corruption. Business schools in China have recently been required to stop admitting politicians into the executive MBA programs for free (Bradshaw, 2014). All too often, some 10% to 15% of the places are reserved for and given to government officials free of charge. The idea was that these institutions would become more attractive to corporate clients and individuals interested in this kind of networking with government officials. Deemed to be a mechanism to promote rather than decrease corruption, China's government was afraid of damaging its reputation. The public should not perceive any furthering of corruption. It does not promote the reputation, credibility, and effectiveness of the business school as a positive societal change agent if it is connected to corruption in any way.

Schools should consider what helps to create a business environment that is more conducive to the greater good and minimizes the risk of perpetuating corruption. Leading by example is key. The president of the European Business School (EBS), Christopher Jahns, who proposed that all graduates take an oath for ethical behavior, was subsequently arrested following allegations of embezzling substantial amounts of funds channeled into his own private firms (Schwertfeger, 2014). He also used school stationery and contacts to get appointments for sales for his private consulting company. The EBS continues to attract attention for its shady practices in generating executive education income, the potential fraud it might be using in its re-accreditation process, and its major lack of transparency (Schwertfeger, 2015). Who would believe that such an institution could create responsible leaders? Would the EBS be a credible, influential provider of holistic leadership education and anti-corruption seminars? Business schools must walk the walk, not just talk the talk. They should be practicing what they preach, without any exceptions.

4.3 Conclusion

This chapter outlines the challenges that confront executive education providers in providing solid and in-depth anti-corruption training within the usual limited allocated timeframes. It also provides methods for addressing these challenges and professionalizing anti-corruption training. The insights shared in this chapter stand as invitations to faculty members, program directors, deans, talent development directors, and other executive education specialists to reflect on additional individual challenges and potential solutions. Business schools can either be silent partners in crime or be the cradle of a new generation of leaders. The thoughts in this chapter should help shift schools toward the latter.

References

Amann, W., Khan, S., Stachowicz-Stanusch, A., & Tripathi, S. (2014). *Innovations in Executive Education*. Borsdorf, Germany: Winterworks.

Amann, W., Tripathi, S. and S. Khan (forthcoming). Driven by customers or driving customers: What really should matter in executive education. In

M.-T. Lepeley, E. von Kimakowitz, & R. Bardy (Eds.). *Human Centered Management in Executive Education: Global Imperatives, Innovation and New Directions*. London: Palgrave McMillan.

Bradshaw, D. (2014, October 19). China's anti-corruption move raises fears for business education. FT.com. Retrieved from www.ft.com/intl/cms/s/2/6f3c82fa-4d6c-11e4-bf60-00144feab7de.html on June 17, 2015.

Gibbs, A. (2014). Chinese corruption worse, despite drive: Report. CNBC. Retrieved from www.cnbc.com/id/102232671 on April 20, 2015.

Phillips, J. (2003). *Return on Investment in Training and Performance Improvement Programs* (2nd ed.) Oxford, UK: Butterworth-Heinemann.

Schwertfeger, B. (2014, October 8). Prozess gegen Ex-EBS-Präsident Jahns vorläufig eingestellt. MBA Journal. Retrieved from www.mba-journal.de/prozess-gegen-ex-ebs-praesident-jahns-geplatzt on 17 June 2015.

Schwertfeger, B. (2015, February 25). EBS: Tricksen für EQUIS? MBA Journal. Retrieved from www.mba-journal.de/ebs-tricksen-fuer-equis/ on June 17, 2015.

Strebel, P., & T. Keys (2005). *Mastering Executive Education: How to Combine Content with Context and Emotion*. Upper Saddle River, NJ: Prentice Hall.

5
Updating the Anti-Corruption Toolkit with locally relevant case studies

In management education, teaching cases are now used worldwide and can be effective in teaching anti-corruption in management education. The Anti-Corruption Toolkit highlights the case method as an important approach. Cases form an essential part of high-impact learning and the sharpening of various skills. They enhance a learner's skills to analyze, apply tools, create and evaluate options, as well as to take and implement decisions. They offer something for all the four learner types identified by Honey and Mumford (1992): activist, reflector, theorist, and pragmatist. While course participants are usually united by their interest in learning and personal growth, they often prefer different ways of learning. An **activist** learner benefits most from activities, interactive, high-speed models, and interactive discussions. A **reflector** prefers observations and subsequent sensemaking, and prefers listening and a slower tempo, along with unrelated questions. A **theorist** draws most from concepts, models, and concrete pieces of information; learning needs to be more structured and discussions need to be focused. A **pragmatist** learns through hands-on experience, enjoys realistic exercises, and needs to understand the *why* and *how* of issues. In the context of anti-corruption education, every type of learner must be acknowledged in a case study. The practical reality and interactive discussions can help to satisfy an activist, while for reflectors, reflective questions can easily be integrated into case discussions. A theorist benefits if each case can be solved within one or more conceptual frameworks, while a pragmatist can work out situation-based answers and seeks opportunities to discuss *why* and *how* questions.

Case teaching is challenging and, therefore, one must be careful when adopting case teaching in anti-corruption-linked management education. Although many professors use cases, they may understand the notion in either a narrow or a broad way. We primarily understand it as a description of a real situation with a protagonist who must make a decision about something. In the context of anti-corruption, this decision is expected to move around the ethical judgment boundaries. A case is a tool to help readers develop independent judgment by being immersed in decision making. A case also helps readers to identify with key managers in the real world. It raises provocative questions and makes readers formulate and defend a point of view and learn through dialectical discussion. All in all, it is a vehicle for good discussion and insight that leads to a clear "lesson."

Cases take different forms, including decision-focused, comparison-contrast, demonstration, or implementation case studies. Lately, another case study type, Mary Gentile's "giving voice to values" (GVV), has become popular. GVV learning methodology relies on decision-making dilemmas through which individuals are trained to speak up at the right point in time and to protect values in critical moments. There are many other types of cases and dilemmas but, irrespective of their form, the cases used in anti-corruption teaching have a common role to play: to educate about anti-corruption effectively in different managerial contexts.

The following sections outline how best to understand and write an effective case, aiming to add fresh insights to recent phenomena and to enhance the local relevance of a taught session. Every faculty member has a choice between "making" and "buying" material. The insights in this chapter can help one to write his/her own cases; this is often faster and advances the school and the faculty's brand more than buying case studies from online case centers. But even when faculty members choose to buy in cases or outsource case writing, there are several points to consider.

5.1 Understanding the core recipe for a case study: the Greek golden rules of storytelling

Cases must be well written if they are to be received positively by an audience. This leads to the question, what are the essential elements of a great case? We suggest that case studies should be built on the Greek golden rules of storytelling, as portrayed in Figure 5.1. Although there are cases that fall outside the norm and still serve a purpose, cases generally involve the following seven elements:

1. **The protagonist.** Each case must be very clear about the perspective to adopt for solving the case. Should an individual – perhaps a mid-level manager or the CEO –

work toward options and choices? Or is it about identifying values in a society and allocating responsibilities
in an economy? A good case clarifies the perspective
from which progress and solutions are to be expected.

2. **The goal.** A case must be straightforward concern-
ing the goals relating to the protagonist, the company
board, or society. This is why cases often end with
key questions; for instance: Should person X decide in
favor of or against plan Y?

3. **The obstacles.** Every case must be clear on at least
some of the obstacles deterring the protagonist and his
or her allies from achieving a goal.

4. **The struggle.** Good cases elaborate on the flow of
events between different episodes, including the origin
of a dilemma as the steps unfold, potentially leading to
a crisis. In cases of corruption, a case should be reasonably clear on the damage that will be caused or may be
expected by decisions to be taken.

5. **The context.** The reader must have sufficient details
about the context in which court decisions must be
taken or in which a dilemma unfolds, for instance, relevant regulations or costs associated with corruption.

6. **The delivery style.** Cases must be well written, in the
active voice, and they should be short enough to ensure
that the reader does not lose interest or develop "paral-
ysis through analysis," i.e., when too much information needs to be processed.

7. **The lessons.** The faculty aiming to use the case must be
clear on the lessons it should bring to the classroom.
Additional ideas might emerge at any point during the

case discussion, but the top three lessons to be conveyed by a case study should be known ex ante.

The last point in the timeline is a case study's natural cutoff point. Beyond positioning a case in terms of the target audience and the complexity level, case authors must decide where to position their cases in a typical decision-making process. While using cases in anti-corruption teaching, these points should be addressed carefully.

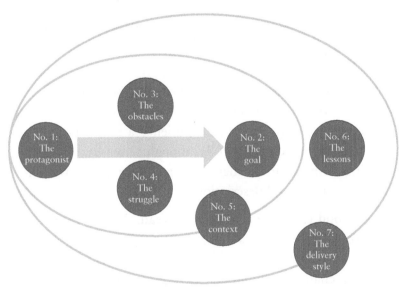

FIGURE 5.1   Elements of the Greek golden rules of storytelling

5.2 Writing anti-corruption teaching cases: some insights

It is best to write a case when the story is fresh – right after the interviews for the case study (for more on how to write good cases, see Adler and Amann, 2011). Time for reflection is crucial, but even days after an interview, many details may already be forgotten. The case then has to rely on secondary material. Fresh cases will motivate course participants more, given people's general interest in up-to-date content. Many published cases in standard textbooks are out of date – the world keeps changing, and the faculty must ensure that students get access to the latest patterns. This also holds true for the selection of case themes. Corruption is a sensitive issue: when the story is fresh, its impact is likely to be high.

There are several definitions of what constitutes a good case. Internationally, there seems to be an emerging consensus on some basic points:

- **A good case shows, it doesn't just tell.** "Show, don't tell" is an oft-cited admonition to writers to write in ways that allow the reader to experience a story through a character's actions, words, thoughts, senses, and feelings rather than through the narrator's exposition, summarization, and description.

- **A good case is not just a good read.** A good case confronts readers with a management issue and, in the case of anti-corruption, a normative management or leadership challenge should be based on a relevant pattern. A case is therefore a story with a teaching purpose. The participants can then contribute to defining or clarifying the issue via discussion.

- **A good case is also a good story.** It is how humans have always communicated – through stories, with embedded wisdom and lessons.

- **A good case follows a strong narrative** with an unexpected or "fresh" opening, a middle that offers just enough background to put the action and case dilemma into context, and a dramatic ending – often a point of no return. A good case is well structured and easy to read. Great cases have clear headlines, a logical buildup, an interesting storyline, and compelling characters. A good case shares more narrative qualities with comic books or short animated films than with research articles or descriptions of business problems.

- **A good case addresses a relevant, important issue.** The issue must be relevant, and it must matter to the audience reading it.

- **A good case is controversial.** If a case gives one nothing to debate, there will be no discussion and no learning. Good cases lend themselves to different interpretations, different judgments, different decisions, and thus different recommended actions. This means that a good case does not demand that the participants merely analyze data and clarify and test their assumptions, but also that they bring their values and principles to bear, and that they question them, too.

- **A good case – and the ensuing discussion – takes readers on a voyage of discovery,** with interesting surprises.

- **A good case keeps skeptical course participants reading, and pushes them to examine their assumptions.** If the participants are unwilling to "suspend disbelief" by leaving their normal world to explore the world of the case and its characters, and if the participants do not struggle with the case data, there will be no learning.

- **A good case contains contrasts and comparisons.** A good case is likely to show the reader different situations, strategies, behaviors, and opinions. Good case writers look for contrasts and comparisons and build them into a case; good case facilitators seek to bring contrasts and comparisons to the fore.

- **A good case has the data the participants need** to address a problem – not too much, and not too little.

- **A good case is authentic.** A good case feels "real"; it is believable. It combines information with emotion and memorable characters. It synthesizes facts and provides the context and perspective – without imposing the author's opinion. At times, it may be necessary to embellish in a case in order to keep the pattern real.

- **A good case creates real "aha moments" for the participants** – surprising insights, new perspectives, and paradigm shifts.

These checkpoints can be useful not only in writing the right cases for anti-corruption education but also for selecting teaching cases appropriate to the context.

5.3 Conclusions

This chapter sought to clarify key insights into writing compelling cases and to give recommendations on how to write case studies so that they become an effective tool that helps to produce interactive and interesting class sessions. Case development does not have to be expensive. Some schools have begun to encourage or require course participants to write cases in order to tailor the content of an executive education seminar, or as part of the submission requirements for a degree program. The research process can also be organized in different ways.

It does not have to be in the form of a paper of 4 to 10 pages; instead, students can submit presentations. What is most important is that the faculty makes an effort to use updated course content that is relevant to specific audiences. Adopting these approaches may help in developing good anti-corruption cases in a very short span of time.

References

Adler, G., & Amann, W. (2011). *Case Writing for Executive Education: A Survival Guide*. Charlotte, NC: Information Age Publishing.

Honey, P., & Mumford, A. (1992). *The Manual of Learning Styles*. Maidenhead, UK: Peter Honey.

6
Developing a common curriculum for integrating the Ten Principles of the UN Global Compact into business education

Corporate concern with sustainability has grown steadily over the last two decades but the linkage between corruption and other sustainability issues has attracted less attention. This chapter argues that an effective sustainability curriculum needs to integrate the other UN Global Compact Principles with the Tenth Principle on Anti-Corruption. This chapter will also provide a way forward for implementation of an integrated sustainability curriculum by focusing on various linkages and relationships between sustainability subjects. Today's business executives operate in complex and challenging environments where global issues such as climate change, poverty, labor rights, and armed conflict shape the business contexts, relationships, and dynamics. They operate in technologically enabled realms of hyper-transparency and with a growing concern for the social, health, and environmental impact of corporations by the general public. For companies to succeed in this interconnected world, managers need to pay attention to issues of social responsibility and sustainability and to see them as integral to achieving their business and commercial objectives. Businesses' strategies and actions on these issues define their contribution to long-term value in society and affect their long-term viability and profitability in the global marketplace.

Corporate concern for human rights, labor standards, environmental projects, and anti-corruption is expanding worldwide. A strategic approach to corporate social responsibility and sustainability produces benefits for companies in the form of corporate reputation, brand loyalty, consumer confidence, employee retention, and regulator goodwill (Glavas and Kelley, 2014; Klettner et al., 2014).

The PRME Anti-Corruption Toolkit highlights a number of these sustainability dimensions and their interlinkages to anti-corruption, transparency and integrity. Teaching and research require careful tailoring of the content without missing the spirit of transparency and integrity in the treatment of the subject matter. Looking at the complexity of the subject, the chapter explores the following issues:

- Why is integration of UN Global Compact Principles needed in the teaching of anti-corruption-related issues?

- What is the conceptual relationship between these sustainability indicators?

- How can we implement the development and delivery of an effective and integrated curriculum?

In the next sections, we will explore these questions by focusing on the discussion of the issues supported by relevant literature and experience-based observations.

6.1 Reasons for integrating the UN Global Compact Ten Principles into management education

The incorporation of the social responsibility and sustainability agenda into company policy and corporate strategy is not just good corporate citizenship; it makes good business sense. Businesses can yield tangible gains in the form of new business opportunities, access to new markets, and reduced transaction costs as they adapt to the preferences and interests of customers and the communities at large.

For example, a coffee company can make a business decision to procure coffee beans picked by growers who manage their crops in a sustainable way and take care to avoid deforestation and erosion. This, in turn, helps in providing local workers with a living wage, in arrangements where profits are reinvested to help preserve the environment and indigenous ways of life. With these practices, the coffee company may advertise its supply-chain relationships as a selling point for the final product. A retail corporation that sets out to work within legal frameworks and honors its own ethical codes is less at risk of being fined for malpractice and less vulnerable to breaches of laws ranging from the violation of labor regulations and environmental standards, to the payment of bribes for which the corporation can be held responsible, its directors indicted, and employees fined for acts of infringement.

Increasingly, companies have found that their sustainability agenda and ethical behavior are strengthening their corporate performance. Among the factors underpinning growing adherence to the sustainability agenda is the reduction of legal risks and avoidance of litigation and indictment, greater freedom from regulation due to more responsible and ethical practices, and greater public acceptance in a transparent marketplace that will expose and censor bad behavior. All these are translated into investor confidence, trust of partners and suppliers, employee morale, and customer loyalty that is motivated and maintained by factors other than cost and quality (Biong *et al.*, 2010). Hence, acting responsibly and behaving ethically is a powerful approach to "doing right" and "doing well" in the business arena.

Business schools must keep pace with the world of practice by broadening their curricula to incorporate the ethical practices and sustainability agenda in order to prepare future generations of managers to succeed in the 21st century. The UN Global Compact has Ten Principles to advance critical issues such as sustainable energy, food and water, women's empowerment, children's rights, and good governance. Over 8,000 companies across over 160 countries have signed up to the Global Compact and have committed themselves to the Ten Principles. One of the Global Compact's sister initiatives, the Principles for Responsible Management Education (PRME), has a number of curriculum development and educational programs aimed at mainstreaming sustainability issues in management education. The Global Compact's Ten Principles and critical issues such as human rights, labor practices, environmental issues, and anti-corruption have so far been addressed separately in focused treatment of each of these issues. For instance, the PRME Workstream on Business for Peace uses applied research to advance business practices that reduce violence and promote justice. The PRME Working Group on Poverty brings together academics and executives to develop strategies and resources to integrate poverty issues and awareness into management curricula and research. The PRME Working Group on Anti-Corruption, the subject of this book, produced the Anti-Corruption Toolkit for educators around the world to access international resources in developing and implementing courses on corruption control.

These different working groups bring together global experts and like-minded organizations and facilitate the in-depth treatment of critical issues of the sustainability agenda in business schools. The PRME Working Groups have already developed resources for each thematic issue such as anti-corruption (the Toolkit), gender equality practices, and poverty-related resources. However, these issue-based approaches to the complex problems are potentially piecemeal and fragmented. They do not engender a systematic and holistic approach to the integration of all the Global Compact Principles into business practices and management education.

Addressing poverty issues or tackling gender inequality in management curricula can make some progress toward the sustainability agenda, but they do not enable management students and business leaders to comprehensively address *all* the major concerns and issues relating to social responsibility and sustainability. When addressed piecemeal in the teaching and research agenda, they may not reveal the strong inter-relationships and dynamics among them. For instance, in real-world scenarios, issues such as poverty, gender discrimination, children's welfare, and minority and migrant rights are interwoven. The rubric of teaching materials and case studies can reflect these inter-relationships and bring out the richness and complexity of real life. See, for example, the case "Never Again – Making Fashion's

Factories Safe." Through presenting, in a case study format, the issues of poverty, forced labor, child labor, gender discrimination, human rights violations, and corruption that plague the clothing manufacturing industries in Bangladesh (War on Want, 2014), it is possible to see the strong inter-relationships. In teaching the impact of corruption, there is growing recognition of the strong connection between corruption and the violation of human rights. Where there is corruption, people are often denied the right to compete fairly in schools, business, and other careers (see, for example, Transparency International, 2009, and U.S. Department of State, 2011). Management practitioners face a world with intertwined issues and dynamics, and students as consumers of management education have growing expectations for teaching in the classrooms to reflect these linkages.

Second, from the perspective of the practice of research, many of the issues such as human rights, labor, environment concerns, food, water, gender, and governance have correlations and causal relationships. For example, it is reported that labor practices (child labor and forced labor) are closely linked to human rights (Environmental Justice Foundation, 2010; ILO, 2009) and labor issues are intricately linked to poverty (de Haan and Yaqub, 2009; Kasente, 2012). It makes sense that management teaching and research address them in a coherent manner. Typically, when conducting studies on the impact of business practices on local communities, risks and impact are considered from the perspective of the stakeholders. These stakeholders experience the risks of corruption, environmental degradation, gender discrimination, and human rights violations as combined, incremental, and cumulative effects, not as disjointed and unrelated problems (Franks *et al.*, 2006). Collecting data on individual issues such as poverty, corruption, and human rights violations on a one-off basis may not truly capture the cumulative effects of the business activities, products, and services and their combined impacts.

For instance, a Human Rights Watch report asserted that the resettlement of thousands of people in Tete Province, Mozambique, between 2009 and 2011 in order to accommodate coal mining operations was a result of regulatory agencies failing to systematically assess the combined and cumulative economic, social, and environmental impacts of the natural resource extraction (Human Rights Watch, 2013).

In the trenches of management practice, business leaders face expectations and pressures from customers, suppliers, regulators, and the community at large, requiring that they address all the ethical issues on the sustainability agenda, not just pick and choose those with which they wish to deal. To advance their corporate objectives, they have to handle the legal, reputational, and financial risks in all sustainability issues, not just a selection of them. An example is the recent mining boom in Mongolia. When the UN's Working Group on the Issue of Human Rights and Transnational Corporations and Other Business Enterprises conducted a study visit to the country, communities provided feedback about the broad impact of companies buying land for mineral exploration on their nomadic grazing lands. They also complained of the related impacts on access to water and how the destruction of the pastureland negatively impacts on the preservation of their culture and lifestyle. With more and more land used for mineral exploration, the communities have to pasture their herds in more remote areas, for longer periods of time, and thus their access to education, health, and other essential social services becomes more difficult and limited (UN Human Rights Council, 2013). The inter-related issues of rights to land and water, access to adequate public services, and changes to the environment mandate a systems approach to corporate responsibility and sustainability.

6.2 Inter-relationship between corporate sustainability indicators

The discussion in the previous section highlights why an integrated sustainability approach is required in teaching and research of anti-corruption issues. One can observe that often the challenges across other sustainability indicators are the result of a lack of transparency and integrity at the execution level. In view of this relationship, a conceptual framework (Amann *et al.*, 2014) explains how the different sustainability dimensions are linked to the transparency, anti-corruption, and integrity dimension, which in turn is conceptualized as a reflection of the behavioral dimension (see Figure 6.1).

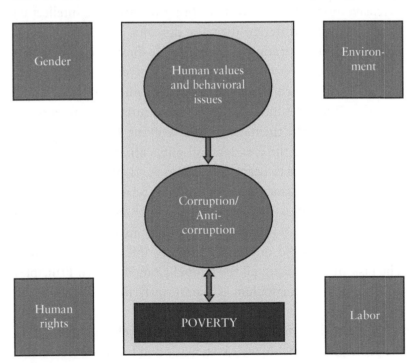

FIGURE 6.1   A conceptual framework inter-relating different sustainability indicators

Source: Amann *et al.*, 2014

6.3 Major challenges in curriculum mainstreaming

As our analyses demonstrate, the need to synthesize these issues and eliminate the overlapping areas prompts the question: how can the UN Global Compact Ten Principles be integrated into one common curriculum? The process of integrating all the sustainability issues of human rights, labor, poverty, gender equality, the environment, and governance in the management program curriculum presents both intellectual and institutional challenges. Synthesizing these broad subjects and critical issues with coherence and relevance in a common curriculum requires extensive research and efforts to bring together the intellectual capital from the different thematic domains. In addition, business education institutions must authorize the curricular changes needed to incorporate sustainability issues in existing courses and educational programming. Efforts to integrate UN Global Compact Principles into the management curriculum are already underway with the thematic PRME Working Groups exploring joint research and the creation and publication of books on the topics. Research has been undertaken (and published) on the nexus of critical issues such as the inter-relationships between poverty and gender, or labor and the environment, or good governance and human rights. These typically involve two themes, and they often yield interesting insights and research findings. The task of integrating all the Global Compact's Ten Principles into a common curriculum is significantly more complex and challenging.

An overarching framework needs to be developed to integrate the principles to enable their systematic and balanced treatment. It is proposed that the framework will consist of three essential components:

1. To provide learning objectives from which educational experiences can be organized to help learners achieve these objectives. This includes the design and sequencing of learning activities, the choice of appropriate teaching methods, and the selection of instructional resources. It answers the question: what learning outcomes are desired for this course to achieve its objectives? Through this objectives-driven process, the course will be oriented to student learning outcomes rather than just the transmission of knowledge or the covering of content. Objectives must be specific and measurable and they need to describe what the learners will know or what they can do as a result of the course activities or instruction. For the purpose of the initiative to integrate the Global Compact's Ten Principles into a common curriculum, learning objectives may include the following:

   – Students will be able to identify the social, ethical, and environmental impact of business strategy and activities.

   – Students will develop strategies, plans, and activities to address issues of human rights, labor rights, the environment, and anti-corruption in the pursuit of business objectives around the world.

   – Students will be able to show sensitivity to the issues of social responsibility and sustainability and be willing to accept responsibility for addressing these issues in the practice of their professions.

2. **To present content-based research and selection of materials to enable educators to prepare lesson plans and teaching notes that are responsive to the needs of learners.** What needs to be covered in the curriculum? What competences are needed by business managers to practice their professions effectively and responsibly?

3. **To provide a way to evaluate the effectiveness of the curriculum.** Evaluation criteria may include the attainment of learning outcomes or the development of abilities deemed essential to meet the educational needs of the students. How do we know the curriculum is delivering to learners what it is designed to do? As the questions of content selection, activities design, and course evaluation are often premised on the wider context of the program objectives, institutional culture, and even the knowledge and discipline of the instructors, only a broad set of guidelines can be proposed. Some examples of the guidelines include the following:

   - **Comprehensiveness.** Does the curriculum comprehensively address all the critical issues on the sustainability agenda of the Global Compact's Ten Principles? The recognition of and commitment to all the principles are critical to the learning process at management schools. A good curriculum includes *all* the Global Compact thematic areas such as human rights, labor, poverty, gender equality, the environment, and governance.

   - **Integration.** Does the curriculum address all the issues in an integrated manner and delve into the correlations and relationships between them? Business executives face a world where these issues do not exist in isolation from one another. Good instructional practice should reflect this reality in order to enhance the relevance of the learning experience.

– **Appropriateness.** Is the introduction and treatment of the issues on the sustainability agenda of the Global Compact's Ten Principles contextually appropriate? Curricular activities must be targeted to the way business school participants learn, and integrated into the discipline's knowledge base and class activities and into the larger school curricula. It must introduce ideas, strategies, and practices in ways that meet the particular needs and interests of students when they enter the world of practice.

6.4 Changing behaviors and reforming systems

The task of developing a common curriculum worldwide for integrating the Global Compact's Ten Principles into business education is a complex but timely challenge. If a common curriculum is to be developed for global application, it must represent the sum of all the best teaching practices and cutting-edge research in the thematic areas and associated fields. A successful curriculum offered by the instructor or the institution integrating the Global Compact Principles has the opportunity to change business strategies and the management practices of generations of executives around the world. Hence, it is critical for the design of learning activities to go beyond the mere "covering of the subject matter" and "transfer of knowledge" to "changing attitudes and behaviors" and "institutional reforms" in order to make a real impact. To this end, customized training materials developed on the Global Compact's Ten Principles must be guided by the purpose of educating future generations of management professionals in the values and competencies of responsible management and ethical decision making.

To achieve this, what do managers need to know? What do they need be able to do? How can an appreciation of the Global Compact's Ten Principles be further translated into a commitment for action? What other skills and values must business school educators impart and cultivate in the students to enable them to truly operationalize the values and practices of global social responsibility and sustainability in challenging business environments? How can business leaders go beyond changing their individual ethical behaviors and choices to influencing organizational environments and practices to sustain ethical practices?

First, an effective response to these questions requires a curriculum that enables well-rounded educational experiences for responsible leadership. An example would be a set of practical skills in undertaking "human rights due diligence," a process recommended by the United Nation's "Protect, Respect and Remedy" policy framework, which ensures that a business respects all human rights and takes all social responsibilities seriously. The framework requires that companies conduct human rights due diligence "to the level commensurate with the risk of infringements posed by the country context in which a company operates, its own business activities and the relationships associated with those activities" (Ruggie, 2008). Such a framework, taught and practiced as part of a course, would build both awareness and knowledge but also the skills required for a broad-based human rights due diligence process that could be applied in different contexts.

In addition, some guiding strategies are needed to make the common curriculum a living, consciousness-raising and empowering approach that will help influence business ethos, strategies, and practices. First, the common curriculum must make a measurable improvement to the business curriculum in terms of the value proposition to learners, instructors, and administrators. It must have the quality of improving the existing curriculum by making it better at preparing students for real-world practice, or strengthening their market competitiveness or employability. This value must be clearly demonstrated to persuade the faculty members and their managers to authorize the expense of time and effort to revise curricula and introduce new materials. For this purpose, the inclusion of sustainability issues and corporate social responsibility alone is not enough. They must be augmented by the benefits of more enrollment in these courses, better course evaluations and learning outcomes, and improved employment opportunities for graduates. These benefits need to be evidence-based and oriented toward motivating instructors to take the first steps toward the uncertain result of changing their curriculum and making the effort of introducing new materials in courses.

Second, the common curriculum must have a focus on not only transferring knowledge and principles, but also imparting skills and competences to business students. The skills are oriented to understanding social, ethical, and environmental impacts but also to strategizing, designing, implementing, and evaluating the effectiveness of social responsibility and sustainability programs. Achieving these learning goals requires the creation of learning activities and environments that enable the effective application of the lessons of the classroom to real-world problems and scenarios. It is one thing to understand the roles, dynamics, and impacts of corporations on social, economic, and environmental value, but it is another to be able to take concrete steps to create these values in highly competitive and complex environments. The ultimate goal of the Global Compact is in moving beyond dialogue and learning to implementation and serious action – designed to make positive and lasting contributions to global human security and sustainability. The test of a company's commitment to the "quadruple bottom line" of economic, environmental, social, and ethical value is its delivery of these values in communities and markets.

Third, the common curriculum must be broadly acceptable to key stakeholders in the business world and in different cultures. Customers, investors, employees, suppliers, regulators, and the media need to be able to support the values and ideas presented in the curriculum. Otherwise, it may not offer significant opportunities for change that is sustainable or scalable, or be able to mobilize collective action coalitions. A common curriculum with broad multi-stakeholder support must also be rooted in ideas and practices that are acceptable in diverse cultures, industries, and business contexts. It should be versatile enough to be acceptable to any business's diverse groups of stakeholders, including investors, stock exchanges, city regulators, professional peers, and clients.

With the above three conditions, it is envisioned that a common curriculum would not only be substantively valuable to business school students, instructors, and administrators, but also one that is politically, socially, and culturally acceptable to key stakeholders and operationally feasible in the business world.

6.5 Conclusion

The rapid expansion of markets, liberalization of trade, globalization, and advancement of technology have greatly expanded the reach and impact of businesses globally. Many countries and corporations, including those operating in the developing world, have been engaged in new economic opportunities in new markets. However, this rapid market expansion and globalization of commerce has also spawned market failures and shortfalls in numerous areas: human rights, labor, gender issues, the environment, and governance. The pace of economic activity has surged ahead of the ability of the political institutions to protect the public good and the competence of local actors and communities to respond and ameliorate the adverse impacts. The sustainability agenda promoted by the Global Compact and PRME is an important milestone in achieving greater alignment between the interests of the international community and the objectives of the business world. A common curriculum integrating the Global Compact's Ten Principles will be yet another step in the global movement to align business operations and strategies to embrace responsible and sustainable corporate policies and practices.

References

Amann, W., Tripathi, S., & Tan, T.K. (2014). *Integrating anti-corruption, poverty and Global Compact Principles in business education curriculum: The way forward.* A presentation at Responsible Management Education Research Conference, Chur, Switzerland.

Biong, H., Nygaard, A., & Silkoset, R. (2010). The influence of retail management's use of social power on corporate ethical values, employee commitment, and performance, *Journal of Business Ethics*, 97(3), pp. 341-363.

de Haan, A., & Yaqub, S. (2009). *Migration and Poverty: Linkages, Knowledge Gaps and Policy Implications*. Geneva, Switzerland: United Nations Research Institute for Social Development.

Environmental Justice Foundation (2010). *White gold, Uzbekistan: A slave nation for our cotton?* Retrieved from ejfoundation.org/sites/default/files/public/ejf_uzbek_harvest_WEB.pdf on January 1, 2015].

Franks, D.M., Brereton, D., Moran, C.J., Sarker, T., & Cohen, T. (2010). *Cumulative Impacts: A Good Practice Guide For The Australian Coal Mining Industry*. Brisbane, Australia: Centre for Social Responsibility in Mining & Centre for Water in the Minerals Industry, Sustainable Minerals Institute, University of Queensland, Australian Coal Association Research Program.

Glavas, A., & Kelley, K. (2014). The effects of perceived corporate social responsibility on employee attitudes, *Business Ethics Quarterly*. 24(2), pp. 165-202.

Human Rights Watch (2013). *"What is a House without Food?" Mozambique's Coal Mining Boom and Resettlements*. Retrieved from www.hrw.org/sites/default/files/reports/mozambique0513_Upload_0.pdf on January 1, 2015.

ILO (International Labour Organization) (2009). *Forced Labour: Coercion and Exploitation in the Private Economy*. Retrieved from www.ilo.org/wcmsp5/groups/public/---ed_norm/---declaration/documents/publication/wcms_112966.pdf on January 1, 2015.

Kasente, D. (2012). Fair trade and organic certification in value chains: Lessons from a gender analysis from coffee exporting in Uganda. *Gender & Development*, 20(1), pp. 111-127. doi: 10.1080/13552074.2012.663627.

Klettner, A., Clarke, T., & Boersma, M. (2014). The governance of corporate sustainability: Empirical insights into the development, leadership and implementation of responsible business strategy, *Journal of Business Ethics*, 122(1), pp. 145-165.

Ruggie, J. (2008). *Protect, Respect and Remedy: A Framework for Business and Human Rights. Report of the Special Representative of the Secretary-General on the Issue of Human Rights and Transnational Corporations and Other Business Enterprises*. Geneva, Switzerland: United Nations Human Rights Council.

Transparency International (2009), *Global Corruption Report 2009: Corruption and the Private Sector*. Retrieved from files.transparency.org/content/download/135/543/file/2009_TIAnnualReport_EN.pdf on January 1, 2015.

UN Human Rights Council (2013), *Report of the Working Group on the Issue of Human Rights and Transnational Corporations and Other Business Enterprises - Addendum - Visit to Mongolia*, A/HRC/23/32/Add.1, para 60. Retrieved from daccess-dds-ny.un.org/doc/UNDOC/GEN/ G13/126/21/PDF/G1312621.pdf?OpenElement.

U.S. Department of State (2011). Country Reports on *Human Rights Practices for 2011: Bangladesh*. Retrieved from www.state.gov/j/drl/rls/hrrpt/ humanrightsreport/index.htm?dlid=186459 on January 1, 2015.

War on Want (2014). *Never Again: Making Fashion's Factories Safe.* Retrieved from www.waronwant.org/attachments/never%20again%20 -%20making%20fashions%20factories%20safe.pdf on January 1, 2015.

7

Anti-corruption teaching and research synchronization

Toward next steps in implementing the Anti-Corruption Toolkit[1]

As discussed in earlier chapters, the fundamental purpose of the Anti-Corruption Toolkit is to help develop management capacity in addressing issues needed for counter-corruption interventions in businesses and organizations. The Toolkit is likely to be implemented across different contexts and over time. This requires dynamic updating of the Toolkit by incorporating knowledge inputs from different contexts; in other words, the

---

1 This chapter is based on Tripathi, S. (2012), Teaching-research synchronization in business schools: A conceptual framework for aligning the research value chain. In W. Amann, M. Kerretts-Makau, P. Fenton, P. Zackariasson & S. Tripathi (Eds.). *New Perspectives on Management Education*. New Delhi: Excel Books.

effective implementation of the Anti-Corruption Toolkit depends on capturing more knowledge about the context in which the management development process takes shape. In view of changing environmental conditions, it also becomes critical to consider how the Toolkit can be made more relevant to existing conditions in a given environment. This raises a further question on the possible role of research in enhancing the scope and relevance of the Anti-Corruption Toolkit while implementing it.

The research function is a critical aspect of management education, since it contributes to knowledge development while also trying to solve managerial issues via systematic information processing. However, there is no uniformity in the research requirements, and one often sees variation in the both the research process and outputs across different institutions. This variation is generally due to the varying requirements of different courses being offered by the institutions at different levels. This equally applies to anti-corruption education in management courses, i.e., the research component for effectively integrating anti-corruption issues in a bachelor-level course in supply chain management may not be same as the research components in a graduate-level course in business environment. Further, the availability of required resources, including human resources, is another factor that can significantly affect the research process in the program into which the Anti-Corruption Toolkit is being integrated. This calls for a sound mechanism for developing the anti-corruption research–teaching synchronization strategy in business schools.

Devising the research strategy for a business-related anti-corruption course is a challenging task, since the existing conventional research paradigm in business schools is more driven by standardized processes and protocols and therefore allows for scope to incorporate the specific requirements of the knowledge area, institution, or context. Can we expect anti-corruption-related research output of a business school operating under challenging environmental and resource constraints to be same as a resource-rich counterpart with favorable environmental conditions? Exploring the answer to this question leads to a fundamental issue of research management processes standardization vs. research outputs standardization. The present scenario of business school research appears to be more influenced by what is considered good research rather than which research type is actually required in the context. While implementing the Anti-Corruption Toolkit, a critical issue is how teaching and research processes can be linked in view of specific requirements. Analysis of this issue raises many questions, including:

- What is the appropriate research output level for further improving the Anti-Corruption Toolkit in a given context?

- Should we integrate research with anti-corruption teaching in business and management courses? Why?

- What are the challenges in designing an effective research strategy for anti-corruption-focused courses?

These questions are the primary focus areas for the present chapter, which suggests a generic framework for aligning the anti-corruption-related research process.

7.1 The dimensions of anti-corruption-related management education

Like the other subject disciplines at higher education level, management education could be conceptualized across the dimensions of teaching, research, and extension/outreach. However, the nature and orientations of activities across these three dimensions vary greatly from the other disciplines, as the knowledge body is multidisciplinary and draws heavily from other subject areas.

Figure 7.1 shows the inter-relationship of conceptual knowledge evolution between the conventional source disciplines and the management subject body. One can see how evolving knowledge from the other disciplines contributes to developments in this particular subject area.

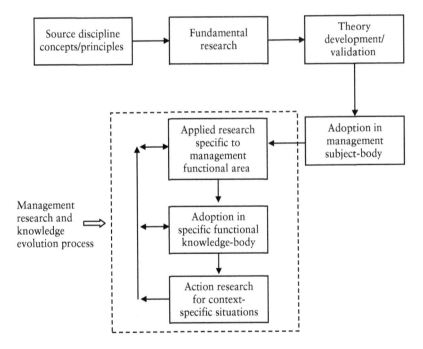

FIGURE 7.1   Inter-relationship in knowledge evolution between source discipline(s) and management

In the specific context of anti-corruption-linked management education, the relationship shown in Figure 7.1 can be explained by an example. Considering the theories on ethical business decision making, we can draw on the knowledge about alternative approaches defined and described in the philosophy of ethics literature, but when the knowledge is adapted to a business course on ethical supply chain management, the research focus shifts to the type of ethical grounds taken by the executives and reasons behind the same.

Conventionally, tertiary-level management education has three major dimensions: teaching, research, and extension. However, the relative positioning of any academic program along these dimensions is determined by a number of factors, which may be summarized under:

- The knowledge–skill development requirement, as derived from the external stakeholder's requirements and stated in the program objectives;

- The extent of dynamism of the academic discipline in terms of knowledge evolution;

- The academic orientations and philosophies of the institutions that design and deliver the programs;

- The objectivity in the process adopted for program development.

This also applies in the context of anti-corruption-related management education. However, the primary issue remains how to decide the teaching and research components while designing and delivering a management course that incorporates Anti-Corruption Toolkit-related issues. The teaching and research activities vary as a process but also complement each other when combined in pedagogy. Further, an anti-corruption course linked to behavior may need more research-based inputs than a course on compliance and reporting. The requirements may also change across the contexts. Given the large number of influencing variables, a fundamental question arises about deciding the right mix of teaching and research in an anti-corruption-linked course. Certainly, there is no single prescriptive model for determining the "right mix" for designing an effective education model, since business schools operate in a fast and dynamic knowledge environment.

7.2 Theory and practice linkages for knowledge co-creation

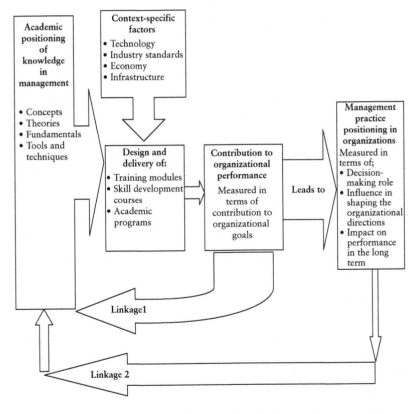

FIGURE 7.2   Knowledge–practice interface in the subject area of management

In view of high potential to influence the direction and degree of research, the theory–practice interface is considered an important issue in management education. Scholars have sought to analyze this issue from different perspectives and in different contexts. Reed (2009) focuses on this issue and suggests that a dialogical rather than a linear model of knowledge production and dissemination is the most analytically and practically useful way of addressing the gap between theory and practice in business and management research.

In his study on the inter-relationships of management with different disciplines, Teece (2011) offers a dynamic capabilities framework that can guide the integration of a curriculum across disciplines and between theory and practice. To understand the dynamics of the theory–research interface in anti-corruption-related management education, we need to look into the different linkages in the process of knowledge evolution that directly or indirectly control the process.

Figure 7.2 conceptualizes the knowledge-development process in the subject area of management from the perspective of theory–practice interface. The model focuses on the primary issue of how knowledge evolution flows from the academic boundaries to the organizational settings and shows the continuous interactions between the two. The same applies to the design and delivery of courses with anti-corruption-related issues. As can be seen, research activities in management are more inclined toward their practical contributions to organizational performance, thereby justifying the relevance focus. On the other hand, academic rigor in the use of analytical methods and tools cannot be ignored when ensuring credibility. Therefore, deciding the specific degree of rigor and relevance at the different levels is another critical area of concern.

Figure 7.2 highlights the research–practice interface in management via two possible linkages, both of which focus on refining the theory and, thereby, practice. However, the scope and impact varies according to linkage type. For instance, at very basic level – shown as Linkage 1 – the primary focus of management research is to fine-tune emerging knowledge in the different contexts. This linkage can be considered important for updating and improving the Anti-Corruption Toolkit. The institutions adapting and implementing the Toolkit will have opportunities to contribute to improve its relevance. The next level – Linkage 2 – aims at generalization and relatively stable knowledge development through repeated experimentation in the different settings. At this level, the focus shifts from testing a specific concept to identifying a common thread that helps to shape further knowledge development. This linkage focuses more on the academic rigor dimension and thus may not be immediately relevant for adapting the Anti-Corruption Toolkit in the near future. A primary challenge for management education is capturing the essence of the needs-based research–practice linkage in the program curriculum to ensure that not only are the students exposed to the issues but that they also develop the capability to analyze practice-oriented research problems in a very objective manner.

The task of aligning the research function with the other value-chain linkages is fraught with challenges. A number of factors may hinder the effective integration of research in the anti-corruption-linked management education process. The nature of organization–institution interface, i.e., the extent of knowledge exchange between the education system and secondary users, is an important factor that influences research positioning. The influence mechanism of both the organization and the education process could be seen as organizations consuming the outputs of business schools and supplying inputs to business schools (Ogawa and Kim 2005). So, aligning the education process value chain with the organization's value chain is one important area for creating an overall values system.

Owing to the increasing market-driven orientation of modern business schools, every institution appears to identify and target the market needs. This gives rise to a fundamental issue of whether to satisfy what the market needs or to focus on strengthening the process capable of delivering changing market needs. A number of scholars agree that business schools are too market driven, focusing too much on rankings and ratings; in this process, the relevance of the research is often ignored. This undermines actionable research and focuses too much on the development of analytical rather than professional managerial skills (Antunes and Thomas, 2007; Ghoshal, 2005; Mintzberg and Gosling, 2002; Thomas, 2007). This gives rise to the potential challenge of convincing the market of the need for anti-corruption-related education – in some contexts, the organizations may fail to perceive the need for it.

The policies and systems in an institution also play a critical role in accomplishing the institution's mission. For instance, when an institution decides to be more relevance focused, it needs internal stakeholder participation in aligning its research function with the perceived strategic position. At this level, the institution would need to channel the efforts of faculty and students to deliver the applied and relevant research outputs. Yet when we look at the appraisal policy in most business schools, research achievements are defined in terms of publication in selected impactful journals, and to get published in scientific journals one needs to focus more on analysis than on relevance. This type of conflicting objective–policy situation may create tension and thus may result in resources being channeled into accomplishing something other than what a value chain needs. In the context of anti-corruption-related issues, this implies that institutions would need to develop an academic incentive strategy that rewarded knowledge creation on anti-corruption issues irrespective of the established accepted knowledge-creation standards.

Another important issue relates to the faculty members' skills sets. We want – and need – the best teachers, the best researchers, the best consultants, and the best academic managers. Considering the nature of the academic process, it is assumed that a good teacher needs to be a good researcher. However, skills requirements vary according to tasks. If we apply this in the context of the academic process, is it justified to expect an individual to develop the competences in multiple task areas? Therefore, the competence requirements and faculty development efforts need to be carefully aligned to what we want to achieve in the research and why. A faculty involved in integrating Anti-Corruption Toolkit issues in its curriculum must be trained and developed to achieve the fine balance between required teaching, research, and knowledge co-creation.

7.3 Research–teaching management to implement the Anti-Corruption Toolkit

Every business school needs a clear, integrated strategy to address the key dimension of research. Therefore, a dynamic framework should be established to determine effective research and teaching coordination in the different courses into which anti-corruption content is being integrated.

A strategic research-process framework is suggested to ensure a balance between rigor and relevance in the research–teaching output of the academic process. The step-wise process shown in Figure 7.3 could be used to position the research according to the context-specific requirements.

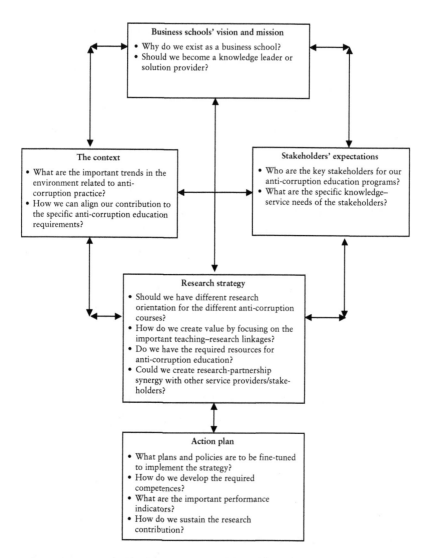

Figure 7.3   Framework for anti-corruption teaching and research process management

The framework aims to develop research management in business schools as a dynamic process with a focus on stakeholders' needs in a given context. The framework does not seek to prescribe a solution but to manage the research process for the effective implementation of a course curriculum based on the Anti-Corruption Toolkit.

7.4 Conclusions

The effectiveness of business school anti-corruption education programs can be ensured by a strong focus on teaching and research dimensions as a complementary and integrated process. A business school academic process primarily depends on the three major dimensions of teaching, research, and extra-professional activities. In anti-corruption-related business and management education, the dynamics of teaching- and research-focused knowledge co-creation becomes vital. However, this process is complex owing to the subject's interdisciplinary nature and the swiftness of its interactions with secondary user organizations. Therefore, conceptualizing and managing the required anti-corruption-related academic process offers a systematic framework to analyze key issues in creating a needs-based anti-corruption education delivery framework. The suggested teaching–research management process aims to mainstream the anti-corruption education in business schools by suggesting possible ways to integrate research and teaching.

References

Antunes, D., & Thomas, H. (2007). The competitive (dis)advantages of European business schools. *Long Range Planning*, 40(3), pp. 382-404.

Ghoshal, S. (2005). Bad management theories are destroying good management practice. *Academy of Management Learning and Education*, 4(1), pp. 75-91.

Mintzberg, H., & Gosling, J. (2002). Educating managers beyond borders. *Academy of Management Learning and Education*, 1(1), pp. 64-76.

Ogawa, R.T., & Kim, R.H. (2005). The business-education relationship: Using organization theory to conceptualize a research agenda. *Journal of Educational Administration*. 43(1), pp. 72-85.

Reed, M.I. (2009). The theory/practice gap: a problem for research in business schools? *Journal of Management Development*, 28(8), pp. 685-693.

Teece, D.J. (2011). Achieving integration of the business school curriculum using the dynamic capabilities framework. *Journal of Management Development*, 30(5), pp. 499-518.

Thomas, H. (2007). Editorial: Strategic themes and challenges facing business schools. *Journal of Management Development*, 26(1), pp. 5-8.

8
Using the Anti-Corruption Toolkit in business schools
Future perspectives

Warren Buffett has famously said that success in business requires three qualities: competence, passion, and integrity; and that without the third, the first two do not count. In other words, ethics and values are an essential part of the business decision-making process. Thanks to Enron, WorldCom, and other famous scandals, business schools are once again paying more attention to ethical issues. There seems to be a pattern emerging in which scandals lead to hype and become forgotten after some 7–10 years. This is when the next scandals happen and history repeats itself. Business schools do not want to be blamed for delivering MBA graduates who are unethical monsters – executives driven only by financial motivation instead of leaders with ethical standards. To address this concern, business schools have introduced ethics courses or modules into their MBA programs – with mixed results. Further, accreditation agencies, such as the Association to Advance Collegiate Schools of Business (AACSB International), now require business schools to incorporate business ethics classes into their MBA programs.

The emerging consensus is that the students have to be (better) prepared for the make-or-break situation, as they will confront a great number of ethical dilemmas in their professional lives. Beyond this common understanding, there is also a debate: what should a business school's educational objective be? Teaching students what it takes not to end their days in jail, or educating businessmen to observe ethical principles beyond the mere legal minimum? Should the focus be on a practical approach (focused on law and rules), or a more abstract approach (focused on reasoning with principles), debating, for example, whether or not there is such a field as "business ethics" as mentioned in Jackson, 2006?

On one point students and teachers agree: students do not want to ruin their careers. It is the duty of business schools to prepare them sufficiently to avoid this fate. But for business schools to recognize this duty is one thing; finding the best way to effectively channel this to students' minds is another much more complex one. It is therefore not surprising that there have been serious discussions on both the optimal ethics curriculum and the teaching methods in academia for years. These conversations are far from over. Thus far, it seems that every business school follows its own recipe. However, business schools and companies should no longer argue that it is already too late to educate their students and employees in ethics, because their ethical compass is formed during childhood through values instilled by family and friends and their primary schools.

There is no definitive answer to the question raised at the end of the second paragraph. Business schools introduce their curriculum in various ways. Some offer stand-alone courses on business ethics of different lengths, ranging from a very few hours in a semester to long full-credit courses. Others prefer a more integrated approach and integrate business ethics into the standard core and functional area course curriculum such as finance, marketing, or corporate governance. The reasoning behind this approach is that ethics and values are part of every business decision. If every business decision has ethical consequences, they have to be discussed in the context of the various business topics where they will be better understood and ingrained than in an isolated ethics course, which might even convey the wrong impression – that business ethics is an isolated topic.

The next level of academic discussion is linked more to the nature of pedagogy: which are the best teaching methods? Teachers use one or more approaches (typically a combination) of traditional, 12-page case studies (plus annexes), lectures, philosophical and sociological text discussions, dilemmas, and role-playing of scenarios based on actual situations. Sometimes instructors use the arts (e.g., movies, theater, literature) to stimulate discussions. Optimally, as many of these methods as possible should be utilized. Lectures and active individual and group participation constitute the backbone of any course taught at business schools today. The Toolkit's chapter on Teaching Methods lists and describes all of them, so they can be chosen to adapt courses and modules to regional preferences and pedagogical needs.

The PRME Anti-Corruption Toolkit's purpose is to help instructors find business ethics and anti-corruption teaching materials most suited to their particular needs and classroom environments. Sims and Felton (2006) have identified four questions to ask when making these choices:

1. What are the objectives or targeted learning outcomes of the course?

2. What kind of learning environment should be created?

3. What learning processes need to be employed to achieve the goal?

4. What are the roles of the participants in the learning experience, especially the roles of the two major players – the instructor and the student?

Business schools typically face serious constraints integrating new courses, or additional sessions, into their existing programs, especially MBA programs. Schedules can be tight and additional time slots for teaching additional classes are slim to non-existent. In order to add content, something else has to be taken out of the program, and the material that is partially, or totally, deleted may include subject matter areas that faculties want to retain. That is one of the reasons why it is so difficult to design a short or long stand-alone course, or even to have a significant amount of classes in different courses dedicated to other teaching objectives. To aid with this process, the Toolkit enables instructors to select materials that meet their needs and interests, and it is a valuable source for teachers who are not ethics or anti-corruption specialists.

One aspect is paramount with regard to education at business schools: it must be praxis-oriented, delivering analytical framework and tools, as well as the required skills on how to confront corruption in real-life situations. Research shows that the most effective training elements are case studies, dilemmas, and, to a certain extent, role-playing. But training has – regardless of its effectiveness as such – much less impact than the organizational support. This insight is of critical relevance for both business schools and companies: the Toolkit's materials are useful for ethics, and anti-corruption education is necessary not just for tomorrow's employees, but also to foster the required organizational support for a strong anti-corruption company culture. These kinds of readings and assignments are also a critical element in leadership curricula in business school and executive education programs, in either a stand-alone or integrated format.

The design and methods for teaching anti-corruption courses are complex. Corruption has many facets that include regional characteristics, as well as sector- and function-specific forms. The Toolkit employs a common ground of subject matter and language to avoid confusion with the implementation in different cultures and work environments (e.g., marketing, finance). To this end, the Toolkit utilizes sources and cases from different continents and both developed and emerging markets. Nonetheless, the Toolkit is sufficiently flexible to enable the instructor to adapt its contents to diverse audiences. Specialized MBA courses will require different designs and teaching methods. For example, executive education is faced with the challenge of adapting methods and contents to different age groups, previous management experiences and positions, and degrees of exposures to corruption. The specific questions to ask are: which teaching methods fit best and whether academics or practitioners with experience of dealing with corruption and its prevention and consequences are best equipped to teach the course.

These two groups may have different approaches. Both are valuable. Used in combination, deep academic analysis and real-life experience with proven tools and strategies can achieve the best possible results. For this reason, the Toolkit recommends vigorous outreach to local business communities to obtain the active participation of experienced and relevant practitioners

(CEOs, compliance officers, etc.). Student exposure to practical experience is essential to business school credibility. Shared professor–practitioner classes tend to be well evaluated by students. The academic instructor contributes theoretical frameworks that are enriched and validated by practitioner experiences with different organizational sectors and levels. The resulting discussions allow the participants to reflect on and build anti-corruption strategies tailor-made to their specific needs. To ensure success, these sessions should be a good mix of lectures, conferences, case studies, dilemmas, and other interactive practices, such as role-playing and simulations. Using these classroom approaches in this order enables the class to evolve from theoretical to practical content and method.

In addition to the Toolkit, there are many additional opportunities to improve their anti-corruption curriculum. Business schools need to actively seek dialogue and regional partnerships with business sector associations and companies. They can also benefit from affiliation with anti-corruption global networks that have local chapters (e.g. UN Global Compact; Transparency International). Developing linkages with the business schools worldwide that have already implemented the Toolkit can also be useful. In so doing, they will obtain helpful advice on how to effectively embed the Toolkit further into their specific regional or industry sectors, and to develop new ideas for a closer cooperation between academia and business. Examples of joint academic–business opportunities include:

- Anti-corruption research centers or anti-corruption chairs: business engagement is essential for quality anti-corruption research. The most successful outcomes have been achieved when business schools have worked closely with executives and have access to company information and data. The Toolkit provides the sources for choosing an adequate framework and body of literature on which to build;

- Assembling best-practice platforms for the exchange of experiences with practitioners (e.g., compliance officers, corporate lawyers, CFOs, etc.): the Toolkit and its global network of participating business schools provide the essential experiences and active support for building these platforms, which have proven extremely useful for fighting corruption in emerging markets with no compliance associations and local networks;

- Developing training sessions and material for developing a code of conduct formulation, an implementation strategy, and effectiveness assessment, as well as websites, videos, game simulations, etc. for specific business sectors, companies, and their value chains. The Toolkit provides a stock of teaching material that should be further adapted to meet regional and local requirements. Business schools, jointly with practitioners, are well suited to do this essential work: the more tailor-made to local situations the teaching material is, the more it will be accepted and taken as a valuable base in class discussions;

- Facilitating collective-action and integrity-pact agreements with specific business sectors or in projects with other stakeholders (e.g., chambers of commerce, non-governmental organizations, and the public sector): in this regard, the Toolkit provides collective-action and integrity-pact sources that business schools can use as building blocks to facilitate agreements that will promote cleaner business-sector niches – especially in emerging markets;

- Organizing conferences and seminars with leading business ethics and anti-corruption experts;

- Helping implement compliance programs and other anti-corruption tools: business schools have expertise in evolving global compliance regimes and their regulatory requirements, which can effectively help companies develop or improve codes of conduct, as well as implement and evaluate compliance programs.

These opportunities will enable business schools to utilize the Toolkit beyond the classroom and contribute to the front-line war against corruption. This will also help in strengthening the Toolkit further with regular dynamic updates. Business schools have a great opportunity to bring academia and business together in ways that enrich and validate academic curricula and research, as well as enhance business practices with broadly applicable concepts.

References

Jackson, K.T. (2006). Breaking down the barriers: Bringing initiatives and reality into business education. *Journal of Management Education*, 30(1), pp. 65-89.

Sims, R., & Felton, E.L. (2006). Designing and delivering business ethics teaching and learning. *Journal of Business Ethics*, 63(3), pp. 297-312.

9
Conclusions

This book has two main goals. The authors aim to improve understanding among fellow deans, program directors, and faculty members about what a modern anti-corruption curriculum could look like and how they could professionalize their own approach in dealing with corruption at their institutions. As outlined in this book, corruption is getting worse in several regions and showing innovative patterns. It might be characterized as an anti-fragile phenomenon, that is, the more sophisticated anti-corruption initiatives become, the faster corruption seems to develop. More research is needed to fully understand corruption and successful anti-corruption effort, particularly in context of management. Likewise, more research is needed to ensure relevant, up-to-date, and localized content for a modern anti-corruption curriculum. In the last chapter, we have discussed possible approaches to align teaching and research in view of dynamic changes in the curriculum.

We have made progress in four areas. First, while we have gained a thorough understanding of many aspects of corruption, new facts and figures along with emerging patterns need to be compiled. The Anti-Corruption Toolkit presents a major effort toward supporting innovative curricula but continuous updating is necessary. Second, the links and interdependencies with other phenomena must be understood better. Third, business schools need more application exercises, and the Anti-Corruption Toolkit contains a selection of ways. Faculty members are encouraged to update themselves continuously. Fourth, the business workload among course participants in business schools is quite high. Even full-time students who do not have to cope with work responsibilities are kept occupied by numerous readings, cases, group meetings, and exams. Reflection on these activities, the content and what it all means for each individual must receive more time in our curriculum. Traditional business schools emphasize knowledge and skills but underperform when it comes to enabling reflection skills and clarifications on what type of manager and leader each course participant actually wants to be. Action is needed to ensure that there is more reflection in business schools.

Professionalizing and constantly updating anti-corruption curricula is a key responsibility of business schools. This is no easy task, even with the support of the comprehensive Anti-Corruption Toolkit and this guide on how to implement it in specific situations because the corruption phenomenon is so complex. We therefore use four complexity drivers to master anti-corruption (outlined in Figure 9.1): **diversity**, **ambiguity**, **interdependencies**, and **dynamics** (flux).

- **Diversity.** At a broader level, there is no single definition or form of corruption – there are various definitions, conceptual frameworks, cause-and-effect relationships, and approaches to remedy, on the individual as well as the organizational level.

- **Ambiguity** complicates analysis and action plans. Headquarters might not know what is culturally accepted and needed to win in remote areas. For example, if a company sponsors a hospital in a country where it intends to build a store, direct bribery does not take place. Local politicians, however, appreciate these efforts and might be more generous when it comes to allocating real estate, granting licenses and so forth. In many cases, ambiguity persists simply because the public may not be aware of the scope of wrongdoing – even with the Internet, which makes news travel fast.

- **Interdependencies.** Developing economies often have to rely on corruption as one of the means of getting things done. Holistic anti-corruption initiatives therefore have to understand the full picture and rely on more than one-dimensional solutions.

- **Dynamics or flux** over time. Corruption evolves at high speed. Corrupt players might well have moved on to new approaches before anti-corruption initiatives that were developed for past problems have been fully deployed.

These four drivers sketch a context around how business schools need to professionalize their anti-corruption curriculum. The Toolkit describes the negative aspects of diversity more fully. As suggested in this book, aligning research and teaching in and across institutions can create positive diversity in the form of varied solutions.

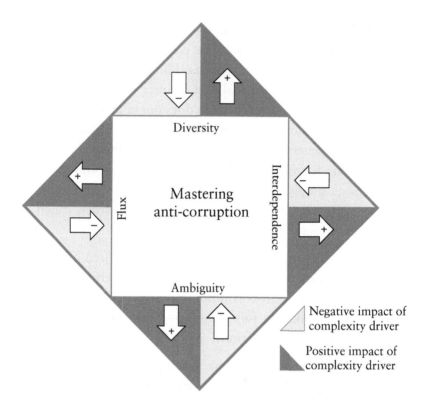

FIGURE 9.1   Complexity drivers in mastering anti-corruption

This is also true for creating positive interdependences in the form of partnerships among business schools and companies for joint learning and other synergies. Providing labor markets with better-trained talents will hopefully deter corrupt players. More knowledge and skills in the business world will clarify ambiguities, making it more difficult for these players to carry out their activities. This will help in developing a momentum to fighting corruption. Learning from best practices internationally on how to implement an anti-corruption curriculum can create positive dynamics, enabling faculty members, schools, and course participants to also work on new ideas.

As such, the outlined framework of the four complexity drivers demonstrates not only why corruption is such a complex phenomenon but also which key drivers to work on when professionalizing anti-corruption initiatives.

All the authors of the Anti-Corruption Toolkit and the members of the PRME Working Group on Anti-Corruption will be available for further discussion on how to better understand corruption and anti-corruption in the management curricula context in the future. Updates will also be available at major PRME events (www.unprme.org) or via the website (actoolkit. unprme.org).

Appendix: Sample syllabus

Carnegie Mellon
Heinz College

Course 90847 information	Corruption, development, and democracy: Theories, policies, and best practices
	Fall 2014 Prof. Emil Bolongaita Email: ebolongaita@australia.cmu.edu This course is delivered simultaneously to classes in Adelaide and Pittsburgh. Due to time zone differences, the classes will be held Friday mornings in Adelaide, and Thursday evenings in Pittsburgh. Due to time zone changes during the semester, class times will also change slightly during the term. Week ADL PGH 8/25/2014 08:30 19:00 8/24/2014 10/9/2014 08:30 18:00 10/8/2014 11/7/2014 09:30 18:00 11/6/2014 Consultation is available by appointment.
Prerequisites	None

Description	Corruption is widely considered to be the single most important obstacle to inclusive economic development and sustainable democratic governance. It is a key factor behind market as well as government failures. Corruption distorts the policy process, privatizes public goods, and deprives the state of resources to address poverty and other economic and social problems. Few countries have successfully tackled the challenges posed by state capture as well as grand and petty corruption. The countries that have effectively done so have reaped governance and anti-corruption dividends that enabled them to attain political, economic, and social benefits for their societies. This course has three objectives. First, it will expose students to the relevant theories and analyses of the impact of corruption and its interactions with development and democracy. Second, it will discuss the range and results of various governance and anti-corruption policies and strategies that have been tried in several countries. Finally, it will analyze the practices of accountability and anti-corruption organizations in select jurisdictions. The underlying goal is to give students a strong foundation for understanding the sources of corruption and enable them to develop and implement approaches that work in different contexts. Case studies of effective and ineffective accountability and anti-corruption organizations will be used.
Course material	Course material will be drawn from book chapters, journal articles, case studies, news reports, videos, and other sources. Course readings **Books** (available in Blackboard) Susan Rose-Ackerman and Paul D. Carrington, eds. *Anti-corruption policy: Can international actors play a constructive role?*, Carolina Academic Press, 2013. Bertram Spector, Michael Johnston, Svetlana Winbourne, *Corruption assessment handbook: Draft final report for US Agency for International Development*, Washington, DC: Management Systems International, 2006. Michael Johnston, *Syndromes of corruption*, Cambridge University Press, 2005. **Articles** – Recommended articles will be available in Blackboard. **The following websites have relevant resource material on corruption and development:** Multilateral development banks World Bank @ www.worldbank.org Asian Development Bank @ www.adb.org European Bank for Reconstruction and Development @ www.ebrd.com Inter-American Development Bank @ www.iadb.org

Islamic Development Bank @ www.isdb.org
African Development Bank @ www.afdb.org

Bilateral development organizations
US Agency for International Development @ www.usaid.gov
UK Department for International Development @
www.gov.uk/government/organisations/department-for-international-development
European Commission (Europeaid) @ ec.europa.eu/europeaid/index_en.htm
Australian Aid @ aid.dfat.gov.au

Other international organizations
International Monetary Fund @ www.imf.org
Organization for Economic Cooperation and Development @ www.oecd.org
(specifically Development Cooperation Directorate @ www.oecd.org/dac)
United Nations Development Program @ www.undp.org

International NGOs
The International Consortium of Investigative Journalists @ www.icij.org/blog
U4 Anti-Corruption Research Centre @ www.u4.no
World Economic Forum @ www.weforum.org
European Network on Debt and Development @ www.eurodad.org
Center for Global Development @ www.cgdev.org
Global Witness @ www.globalwitness.org
Transparency International www.transparency.org

Recommended books:

Robert Klitgaard, *Controlling corruption*. University of California Press. 1988.

Arnold J. Heidenheimer and Michael Johnston, eds. *Political corruption: Concepts and contexts*. Transaction Publishers, 2002.

Carolyn Nordstrom, *Global outlaws: Crime, money, and power in the contemporary world*. University of California Press, 2007.

Bertram I. Spector, ed. *Fighting corruption in developing countries: Strategies and analysis*. Kumarian Press, 2005.

Hilton L. Root, *Capital and collusion: The political logic of global economic development*. Princeton University Press, 2006.

Frank Anechiarico and James B. Jacobs, *The pursuit of absolute integrity: How corruption control makes government ineffective*. University of Chicago Press, 1996.

	Steven Kelman. *Procurement and public management: The fear of discretion and the quality of government performance*. AEI Press, 1990. Yan Sun, *Corruption and market in contemporary China*. Cornell University Press, 2004. J. Edgardo Campos, ed. *Corruption: The boom and bust of East Asia*. Ateneo de Manila University Press, 2001. Jon S.T. Quah, Curbing corruption in Asia: A comparative study of six countries. Eastern Universities Press, Simon S.C. Tay and Maria Seda, eds. *The enemy within: Combating corruption in Asia*. Eastern Universities Press, 2003. Peter Lilley, *Dirty dealing: The untold truth about global money laundering, international crime and terrorism*, Kogan Page, 2003. Vinay Bhargava and Emil Bolongaita, eds. *Challenging corruption in Asia: Case studies and a framework for action*. World Bank, 2004.
Evaluation method	The final grade will be based on four areas: class participation and presentations (40%), a mid-term paper (30%), and a final paper (30%). The mid-term paper will be an analysis of corruption in a particular country, sector, or organization. The final paper will extend the analysis in the mid-term paper and propose recommendations on how to tackle corruption in the selected country, sector, or organization.

Learning objectives	Learning objective	Assessment method
	Demonstrate understanding of theories and analyses of the impact of corruption and its interactions with development and democracy.	Class participation and presentations, mid-term paper, final paper
	Demonstrate knowledge of various governance and anti-corruption policies and strategies that have been tried in several countries.	Class participation and presentations, mid-term paper, final paper
	Demonstrate ability to develop and implement best practices in accountability anti-corruption organizations	Class participation and presentations, mid-term paper, final paper

Grading scale							
	A+	99.0-100%	B+	88.0-90.9%	C+	78.0-80.9%
	A	94.0-98.9%	B	84.0-87.9%	C	74.0-77.9%
	A-	91.0-93.9%	B-	81.0-83.9%	C-	71.0-73.9%

Course Outline		Class 1
	Topic	**Introduction: Corruption, development, and democracy**

	Class 2	
Topic	**Corruption: Overview**	
Readings	Michael Johnston, *Syndromes of corruption*, chapters 1-2. Robert Klitgaard, "A holistic approach to fighting corruption," 2008 Vito Tanzi, "Corruption around the world: Causes, consequences, scope and cures," International Monetary Fund, 1998	
Guide questions	What is corruption? What are its causes? What are its consequences?	

	Class 3	
Topic	Corruption: Types and trends	
Readings	Michael Johnston, *Syndromes of corruption*, chapter 3. Case study: China Yan Sun, "Corruption, growth and reform: The Chinese enigma," *Current History*, September 2005 "Corruption: No ordinary Zhou," *The Economist*, 2 August 2014, www.economist.com/news/china/21610313-carrying-out-most-significant-purge-generation-xi-jinping-seeks-tighten-his-grip-no "Corruption and the economy," *The Economist*, 2 August 2014 www.economist.com/news/china/21610316-weighing-economic-impact-anti-corruption-campaign-anti-graft-anti-growth.	
Guide questions	What are the different types/kinds of corruption? Why is corruption in China an enigma?	

Class 4 (ADL: Sep 19th, PGH: Sep 18th)	
Topic	Corruption: Perceptions versus reality
Readings	Transparency International, *Corruption Perceptions Index 2013*, at www.transparency.org Transparency International, *Bribe Payers Index 2011*, at www.transparency.org Transparency International, Global Corruption Barometer 2013, at www.transparency.org Case study: Australia Organization for Economic Cooperation and Development, *Report on Implementing the OECD Convention on Bribery in Australia*, at www.oecd.org ABC News, "Australia 'failing' to tackle bribery by multinational companies: OECD," at www.abc.net.au/news/2014-01-06/australia-accused-of-failing-to-tackle-bribery-among-multinatio/5187070.

Class 5	
Topic	**Investigating and prosecuting corruption**
Readings	Tony Kwok, "Investigation of corruption cases" Sheila Coronel, "How to track looted wealth," at www.icij.org/resources/how-track-looted-wealth. Sheila Coronel, "Eight ways to commit grand corruption (parts 1 and 2)," at watchdog-watcher.com/2012/06/21/8-ways-to-commit-grand-corruption-part-1/?blogsub=confirming#blog_subscription-3 (part 1); watchdog-watcher.com/2012/06/29/8-ways-to-commit-grand-corruption-part-2 (part 2) "Thousands of officials punished," China Daily, January 11, 2014, at www.chinadaily.com.cn/china/2014-01/11/content_17229794.htm. "Mistakenly-released report reveals embarrassing extent of Chinese corruption," *The Australian*, June 17, 2011, at www.theaustralian.com.au/news/world/accidentally-released-report-reveals-embarrassing-extent-of-chinese-corruption/story-e6frg6so-1226076938605.

Class 6	
Topic	**Anti-corruption agencies**
Readings	Emil Bolongaita, "An exception to the rule? Why Indonesia's anti-corruption commission succeeds where others don't – a comparison with the Philippines' ombudsman," U4 Issue, Chr. Michelsen Institute, 2010. John S.T. Quah, "Anti-corruption agencies in four Asian countries," Paper presented at 6th Asian Forum on Public Management on comparative governance reform in Asia, January 2007. John R. Heilbrunn, "Anti-corruption commissions: Panacea or real medicine to fight corruption," World Bank, 2004.

Class 7	
Topic	**Corruption and democracy (Focus: Latin America)**
Readings	Moises Naim, "Mafia states: Organized crime takes office," *Foreign Affairs*, May-June 2012. Juan Carlos Zuleta, "Combating corruption in the revenue service: the case of VAT refunds in Bolivia," U4 Brief, Chr. Michelsen Institute, 2008. Gustavo Coronel, "Corruption, mismanagement and abuse of power in Hugo Chavez's Venezuela," Center for Global Liberty and Prosperity, November 2006. Francis Fukuyama, "Democracy and corruption," blog post, October 2012, at www.the-american-interest.com/fukuyama/2012/10/05/democracy-and-corruption (also see previous blog post at www.the-american-interest.com/fukuyama/2012/10/02/the-strange-absence-of-the-state-in-political-science)

Deadline for mid-term paper: Friday, October 17

Class 8	
Topic	**Corruption and development (Focus: South Asia)**
Readings	Nathan Associations, "USAID anti-corruption interventions in economic growth: Lessons learned for the design of future projects," June 2006. Nathaniel Hobbs, "Corruption in World Bank financed projects: Why bribery is a tolerated anathema," Working paper No. 05-65, London School of Economics, December 2005. "Fighting corruption in India: A bad boom," March 15, 2014, *The Economist*, at www.economist.com/news/briefing/21598967-graft-india-damaging-economy-country-needs-get-serious-about-dealing-it I paid a bribe website www.ipaidbribe.pk

Class 9	
Topic	**Corruption and money laundering (Focus: China, Vietnam)**
Readings	Roberto Michele, "How can international financial institutions support countries' efforts to prevent corruption under international treaties and agreements?" in *Anti-corruption policy: Can international actors play a constructive role?* Indira Carr and Robert Jago, "Corruption, money laundering, secrecy and societal responsibility of banks," Social Science Research Network, June 2014. OECD resources on money laundering, at www.oecd.org/cleangovbiz/toolkit/moneylaundering.htm

Class 10
Topic	**Corruption: Business and government (Focus: Wall Street)**
Readings	Ernst & Young, "Building a more ethical business environment: Asia-Pacific Fraud Survey 2013." Labaton Sucharow, "Wall Street in crisis: US financial services industry survey," July 2013. George Packer, "A dirty business: New York City's top prosecutor takes on Wall Street crime," The New Yorker, June 27, 2011 at www.newyorker.com/magazine/2011/06/27/a-dirty-business New York Times, "Preet Bharara's key insider trading cases," July 18, 2014, at www.nytimes.com/interactive/2014/07/09/business/dealbook/09insider-timeline.html?action=click&contentCollection=N.Y.%20%2F%20Region&module=RelatedCoverage&region=Marginalia&pgtype=article#/#time337_8872

Class 11
Topic	**Corruption in procurement (Focus: Military)**
Readings	Paul R. Schapper, "Corruption and technology in public procurement," A report prepared for the World Bank, April 2007. Sam Perlo-Freeman and Carina Solmirano, "Why arms procurement goes wrong," Stockholm Peace Research Institute. "Modi eases graft-linked curbs to spur arms deals in India," BloombergBusinessweek, September 16, 2014, at www.businessweek.com/news/2014-09-15/modi-eases-graft-linked-curbs-to-spur-arms-deals-in-india

Class 12
Topic	**International actors and corruption (Focus: International organizations)**
Readings	Jana Kunicova, "The role of the World Bank in promoting good governance and anti-corruption reforms: A view from Europe and Central Asia region," Chapter 2, in *Anti-corruption policy: Can international actors play a constructive role?* James P. Wesberry, "International financial institutions face the corruption eruption," *Northwestern Journal of International Law and Business*, Winter 1997. Joseph Stiglitz, "Corrupting the fight against corruption," Project Syndicate, at www.project-syndicate.org/commentary/corrupting-the-fight-against-corruption

Class 13	
Topic	**International actors and corruption (Focus: Private sector, NGOs)**
Readings	Robin Hodess, "Civil society and nongovernmental organizations as international actors in anti-corruption advocacy," in *Anti-corruption policy: Can international actors play a constructive role?* Ethan S. Burger and Mary S. Holland, "Why the private sector is likely to lead the next stage in the global fight against corruption," *Fordham International Law Journal*, vol. 30, issue 1, 2006.

Class 14	
Topic	**Conclusion: In pursuit of performance, results, and integrity**
Readings	Michael Johnston, "From analysis to reform," Chapter 8, in *Syndromes of corruption*.

Deadline for final paper: December 11, 2014

Plagiarism and cheating notice	Plagiarism and other forms of academic misrepresentation are taken seriously. Misrepresentation of another's work as one's own is regarded as among the most serious violations. The violation is flagrant when it occurs as plagiarism in a required paper or assignment or as cheating in an examination, regardless of whether it is a take-home or in-class examination. The punishment for such offenses can involve expulsion from the program. *Academic dishonesty:* Students are expected to maintain the highest ethical standards in and outside the classroom. Cheating on exams and term papers (e.g., plagiarism and unauthorized collaboration) will be treated strictly. The usual penalty for violations is a failing grade for the assignment in question; however, in some instances such actions may result in a failing grade for the course.
Course policies and expectations	Attention to detail is prized in this course, particularly in presentations and written assignments. This includes attention to spelling, formatting, and other instructions. Punctuality in class attendance and submission of requirements is also valued. Respect for and openness to each student's contributions are deemed crucial to the mutual learning objectives of the course. Rules and examples will be discussed at the start of the course to underscore the importance of these guidelines. The professor will handle the course as a discussion leader and senior colleague, not as an infallible instructor or an authority who may not be challenged. Different or dissenting views are welcome and are in fact encouraged, subject to the dictum of mutual respect and openness. The professor will appreciate questions and suggestions in actual and virtual discussions. This will help underpin the course values of transparency, fairness, and accountability, which are essential to engendering shared responsibility and high standards in addressing critical problems in international development.

Contributor biographies

The following experts have contributed to the Anti-Corruption Toolkit:

Wolfgang Amann graduated from Harvard University's Institute for Management and Learning in Higher Education. He learned his research skills at The Wharton School of the University of Pennsylvania in Philadelphia and his executive education skills at IMD in Lausanne. After years in top management consulting, he has been marketing, designing, directing, and delivering executive education seminars, as well as MBA programs, for more than a decade. He has also been a visiting professor in the field of international strategy and sustainability at Hosei University in Tokyo, Tsinghua in Beijing, the Indian Institute of Management in Bangalore, ISP St. Petersburg in Russia, Warwick Business School, and Henley Business School in the UK. He now serves as professor of Strategy and Leadership, as well as Academic Director, of several degree and custom programs at HEC Paris in Qatar.

Ronald E. Berenbeim is an adjunct professor at the New York University Stern School of Business Administration, where he has taught Professional Responsibility: Markets Ethics and Law since 1995. He is also a senior fellow at The Conference Board. From 2001 to 2003, he was a project director for a World Bank study of private sector anti-corruption practices in East Asia. He currently serves as director of The Conference Board and World Bank project on Trade Competitiveness and Integration of Poor Countries in Global Supply Chains. He is a member of the Global Compact Tenth Principle (anti-corruption) Working Group, Transparency International's Steering Committee on Business Principles for Resisting Corrupt Practices, and the US Advisory Board of FTSE4Good. In 2010, he received a Fulbright grant to teach business ethics and governance at the University of Cergy-Pontoise, France. In 2011, he was selected by Trust Across America as one of 2010's Top 100 Thought Leaders in Trustworthy Business Behavior. Ronald is a graduate of Cornell University, Balliol College, Oxford, and Harvard Law School.

Gabriel Cecchini is Coordinator of the Center for Governance and Transparency at IAE Business School in Buenos Aires, Argentina. He has a BA in Communication from the National University of Cordoba in Argentina, an MA in Social Sciences (Sociology) from the University of Chicago and has started a PhD in Sociology at the Catholic University of Leuven in Belgium. He has joined research projects on the area of philosophy of the social sciences and social theory, specializing in functional differentiation theory and the work of Niklas Luhmann. He is currently coordinating research for and support of companies in the field of compliance, anti-corruption, and best practices at IAE's Center for Governance and Transparency.

Dominic DePersis is professor of Business Law and International Business. He is an instructor of business law, contract law, ethics and health policy, international law and business, and hospitality law at the undergraduate level. He studied under the guidance of the protégé of the founding father of strategic management, Professor H. I. Ansoff. Dominic has an extensive background in teaching, research, grant administration, and law practice. He has had the privilege to practice law in New York, Minnesota, New Jersey, and the District of Columbia. He has lectured internationally, including in Russia, Ukraine, and Taiwan. He has published numerous articles in the fields of law, the philosophy of jurisprudence, and management. Dominic has co-led several international grants. He serves on several boards. He holds a BS 1995, Binghamton University; JD 1998, Syracuse University; SJD 2005, Northwestern California University. His research interests include international law, anti-corruption laws, jurisprudence, not-for-profit institutions, and human rights.

Mary C. Gentile is Director of Giving Voice to Values and a senior research scholar at Babson College; senior adviser of the Aspen Institute Business & Society Program; and an independent consultant. Previously, she was a faculty member at Harvard Business School (1985-95), where she was one of the principal architects of the innovative educational program, Leadership, Ethics and Corporate Responsibility. She co-authored *Can Ethics Be Taught? Perspectives, Challenges, and Approaches at Harvard Business School* (with T.R. Piper and S. Parks, Harvard Business School Press, 1993). Other publications include *Differences That Work, Managing Diversity, Managerial Excellence Through Diversity: Text and Cases*, and numerous articles, cases, and book reviews. She served as content expert for the award-winning interactive CD-ROM, Managing Across Differences (Harvard Business School Publishing, 1996). She holds a bachelor's degree from The College of William and Mary (Williamsburg, VA) and an MA and PhD from the State University of New York.

Jonas Haertle is Head of the Principles for Responsible Management Education (PRME) Secretariat at the United Nations Global Compact Office. He is responsible for driving the mission of the PRME initiative, to inspire responsible management education, research, and thought leadership globally. Jonas holds a Master's degree in European Studies from Hamburg University. As a Fulbright scholar, he also obtained an MSc degree in Global Affairs from Rutgers University in the USA. He provides global leadership in bringing together good practice in implementing the principles of PRME and the Global Compact. He has collaboratively hosted and participated in PRME forums in Asia, Europe, and other regions of the world.

Christian Hauser is a professor of Business Economics and International Management at the Swiss Institute for Entrepreneurship (SIFE) at the University of Applied Sciences, HTW, Chur. He studied Latin American Studies at the universities of Cologne (Germany), Lisbon (Portugal), and Fortaleza (Brazil). In 2006, he gained his doctorate in Economics on Foreign Trade Promotion Schemes at the University of Cologne.

During his PhD studies, he worked at the Center for the Portuguese Speaking World at the University of Cologne. In 2006, he joined the Institute for SME Research (IfM) Bonn as a postdoctoral research associate. Since July 2007, he has been working at the SIFE on topics that include international entrepreneurship, SME and private sector development, and business integrity.

Polina Kalnitskaya is an independent consultant on corporate governance and business ethics. She is an external consultant for the International Business Leaders Forum for developing a business ethics course for Russian educational institutes. Polina has been teaching corporate governance and ethics in Moscow International Higher Business School MIRBIS. Her legal experience started in 1995 and she was a legal adviser of the IFC/World Bank projects "Corporate Governance in Russia" and "Corporate Governance in the Banking Sector of Russia" (2001–2007), and also the EU/TACIS project "Corporate Governance in Russia" (2005). She also worked as the Consulting Director for Russian National Independent Directors Association until 2010 and is a certified organizational gestalt-consultant and business trainer. She is a graduate of the Southern Federal University and Institute of Management, Business, and Law (Russia).

Matthias Kleinhempel served as a full-time professor at IAE Business School from 1999 to 2002. In 2009, he rejoined IAE and currently teaches in the MBA and the Executive Education programs. He is the Director of the Center for Governance and Transparency at IAE and the Academic Director of the Senior Executive Program Latin America in Miami. He holds an MBA degree from IAE and a law degree from the University of Hamburg, Germany. His research deals with corporate governance, business ethics, and regional strategies. He is a visiting professor at IESE Business School. In the past, he served in a number of positions at Siemens: he was President and CEO of Siemens Venezuela, CFO of the Andean Region, President of the Cable Division (with responsibility for worldwide business), and CEO and President of Siemens in Argentina and CFO of the Mercosur Region.

Hans Krause Hansen is a professor of Governance and Culture Studies at Copenhagen Business School. Originally trained in political science and Latin American studies, his current research revolves around the role of private actors in global governance, anti-corruption practices in international business, and the surveillance infrastructures, organization, and practices of transparency regimes. Hans has published in journals such as the *Bulletin of Latin American Studies*, *Gestión y Política Pública*, *Critical Quarterly*, *Citizenship Studies*, *Alternatives: Local, Global Political*, *International Studies Review*, *Review of International Political Economy*, *Journal of International Relations and Development*, *International Political Sociology*, and *Crime, Law, and Social Change*, and contributed to a wide range of international anthologies. Hans previously served as Academic Director of the Business, Language, and Culture Studies Program at CBS, and he is currently head of the Doctoral School of Organisation and Management Studies, CBS. He is a member of the PRME Working Group on Anti-Corruption.

Alfred Lewis is professor of Management and Economics, School of Business, Hamline University. Alfred is an award-winning instructor of finance, international business, and strategic management. He studied under the guidance of the founding father of strategic management, Professor H.I. Ansoff. He has published numerous books and articles in the field of banking, entrepreneurship, not-for-profit management, law, international business, and strategic management. Given the increasingly global economy, Alfred has led numerous study-abroad programs. He serves on several editorial boards and is editor of the journal *Business Strategy Series* and the associate editor of the *British Journal of Management & Economics*. Alfred holds a BS from the American International University, England, an MBA and DBA from International University, United States, and an EJD from Concord Law School. His research interests include banking, corporate strategy, not-for-profit institutions, and political economy.

Daniel Malan is a Senior Lecturer in Ethics and Governance at the University of Stellenbosch Business School (USB) and Director of the Centre for Corporate Governance in Africa at the USB. His focus areas are corporate governance, business ethics, and corporate responsibility. He is a member of the World Economic Forum's Global Agenda Council on Values in Decision Making, the International Corporate Governance Network's Integrated Business Reporting Committee, and the PRME Working Group on Anti-Corruption. His educational qualifications include a Masters degree in Philosophy and a Masters degree in Business Administration (MBA), both from the University of Stellenbosch in South Africa.

Ruth Nieffer studied Sociology, History, Art and Media Science at the University of Konstanz, Germany and has a Master's degree in Sociology (MA). While working for a number of non-profit organizations she completed a training program in Vocational and Adult Education (Swiss Federation for Adult Learning). She also undertook a Master of Advanced Studies Program in Business Psychology at the University of Applied Sciences and Arts, Northeastern Switzerland. Ruth works as a project leader and researcher at the Swiss Institute for Entrepreneurship (SIFE) at the University of Applied Sciences Eastern Switzerland at Chur. Her research interest focuses in Business Integrity, Corruption in SME and Anti-Corruption/Compliance Training. She teaches basics in Psychology and Communication and an Ethics module in the bachelor degree program in Business Administration.

David Odrakiewicz is an economist, originally from Canada, but with Polish roots and educated in Scotland (University of Aberdeen). David is interested in the interplaying areas of economics, efficient management, integrity competences, entrepreneurship, and corporate social responsibility. He combines his research interests with internships he completed at Santander Bank and DM BZWBK Brokerage House, his position in the AMEX company as CSR manager in marketing, and management trainer and competence educational consultant for youths at the GPMI Research Institute with offices in Poznan, Aberdeen, and Vancouver.

Peter Odrakiewicz is an adjunct professor at Poznan PWSB and visiting professor at Romania/Partium Christian University. He is a research fellow and the director of Evolute Programme (Finland, USA, Korea, and international). He is the Dean of Managerial Linguistics at Poznan PWSB/Poznan University College of Business, was Vice-Rector from 2007 to 2011, visiting professor multiplex, and director of the International Management Program at the Department of Economics and Management. In addition to his academic duties, Peter was appointed to the board of AMEX PPHU, previously worked at the DaimlerChrysler Canada, Inc. headquarters, and is an innovator, leading teacher, author, co-author, and editor of more than eight scientific books. He has presented numerous academic research papers including for Rotterdam School of Management Erasmus University, EDINEB Vienna, and Chicago and Montreal AOM conferences, and is a reviewer at the Academy of Management, USA.

Kemi Ogunyemi teaches Business Ethics, Anthropology, and Sustainability Management at the Lagos Business School, Lekki campus, of the Pan-African University. She holds a law degree (University of Ibadan), an LLM (University of Strathclyde), and an MBA (Lagos Business School). After law school, she worked as director, team lead, and mentor in projects for the Women's Board (Educational Cooperation Society) before she joined Lagos Business School. In these roles, Kemi has coordinated and facilitated numerous courses on character formation and personality development. She has also contributed to international publications on respecting diversity and teaching values, and has authored journal articles and teaching cases. She is a member of the PRME Working Group on Anti-Corruption and of the EBEN SIG on Teaching Business Ethics.

Roberta Paro has a degree in Agricultural Engineering (University of the State of São Paulo, Brazil, 1996) and a Master's degree in Environmental Science (Lund University, Sweden, 2000). As associate professor and researcher at the Center for Corporate Sustainability at Fundação Dom Cabral since the end of 2005, she has coordinated research on the incorporation of sustainability into strategic planning and corporate governance, and developed tools, cases, and studies on the integration of sustainability challenges into business. She is a member of the PRME Working Group on Anti-Corruption. Previously, she worked at the Ethos Institute of Business and Social Responsibility (2002–2003) and as a teaching assistant and project assistant at Lund University. Roberta was an invited teacher at Malmö University (2001) and for the postgraduate course on CSR at the business school Fundação Getúlio Vargas FGV-EAESP (2002).

Ajai Prakash is connected to the Department of Business Administration, University of Lucknow, India. He is a visiting researcher at ISAE, Brazil, and other institutes. He teaches strategic management and international business, and is a recipient of the Career Award for Young Teacher from the All India Council of Technical Education. He was educated at Lucknow and holds a PhD in Business Administration, MBA, and LLB. He started his career as an academic at the University of Lucknow. He had a short stint with IIM Lucknow before joining KCA University, Nairobi, Kenya, where he was a professor, and dean of the School of Graduate Studies.. He was the first director of B.Com (Hons.) and assistant director of the Planning and Development Board, University of Lucknow. His interests are anti-corruption, poverty, and social change issues in the Indian Subcontinent and East African region. He works with PRME Working Groups on Poverty and Anti-Corruption.

Agata Stachowicz-Stanusch, PhD, DSc, associate professor of Management, Silesian University of Technology, Poland, is head of the Management and Marketing Department. Next to many articles, she has written 14 books including *Integrity in Organizations: Building the Foundations for Humanistic Management* (Palgrave Macmillan, forthcoming), *Business Integrity in Practice* (Business Expert Press, forthcoming), and *Education for Integrity: Handbook of Research on Teaching Ethics in Business and Management Education* (IGI Global, 2012). She is a World Engagement Institute and International Fellow, Chief-of-Research of the International Higher Education Teaching and Learning Association, member of the Anti-Corruption Academic Initiative, and a member of the Polish Academy of Sciences, Committee on Organizational and Management Sciences. Other recent services include being a track chair for EURAM conferences, PDW co-organizer and presenter for the AOM Annual Meeting in San Antonio (2011). She is a co-founder and vice editor-in-chief of the *Organizational and Management Journal* and a member of many editorial boards.

Tay Keong Tan is Director of International Studies and Associate Professor of Political Science at Radford University in Virginia, USA. He teaches courses in international studies and political science and focuses his research on anti-corruption and governance. He is a Fellow at the Institute of Policy and Governance at Virginia Tech. Dr. Tan has been the principal investigator of a number of projects on governance reforms in Virginia funded by the Jessie Ball DuPont Foundation and Radford University, on the issues of ethics, and nonprofit leadership and governance. A member of the Principles for Responsible Management Education (PRME), he is co-editor of a book with a theme on global sustainability, *Beyond the Bottom Line: Integrating the UN Global Compact into Management Education*, to be published in 2016 by Greenleaf Publishing. Dr. Tan has a doctorate in Public Policy from Harvard University's Graduate School of Arts and Sciences and a Master's degree in Public Policy from the Harvard Kennedy School.

Davide Torsello, social anthropologist, is an associate professor at CEU Business School, Hungary. He is also senior researcher at the Center for Integrity in Business and Government, CEU Business School. His main interests concern the study of corruption, in both private and public sectors, from a social and cultural perspective. He is the coordinator of a work package entitled The Ethnographic Study of Corruption, part of a major EU FP7 cooperation grant that includes 21 institutions. He has published seven books and over 30 articles on issues including corruption, trust in institutions, social networks, informal exchange, and postsocialism. His latest book, *The New Environmentalism? Civil Society and Corruption in the Enlarged EU,* has been published by Ashgate (2012).

Shiv K. Tripathi is a professor at Mzumbe University, Dar Es Salaam School of Business, Tanzania. He teaches strategy, operations, supply chain, and ethics courses. He received his doctorate from Mahatma Gandhi Kashi Vidyapith (Varanasi, India) for his work on comparative management thoughts of the East and the West. He is an alumnus of IESE Business School (Spain). Before joining Mzumbe University in 2009, he was dean of the Faculty of Management Studies at VBS Purvanchal University (India). His research interests include strategic management applications, ethics in management, and higher education management. He has conducted sponsored research projects in strategic higher education management, and is associated with a number of international journals and professional bodies as a reviewer and editorial board member. He initiated a Special Cell on Human Values and Ethical Management at VBS Purvanchal University and organized conferences and workshops on human values-oriented management. He is a member of two PRME Working Groups.

Bertrand Venard is a professor of Strategy at Audencia Nantes School of Management (France). He received a doctorate in Management and postdoctorate diploma from the University of Paris. He previously worked in the financial industry and for PricewaterhouseCoopers. He has held various administrative positions in higher education, including dean of a business school in Vietnam. He has been a visiting professor at The Wharton School of the University of Pennsylvania, London Business School, University of Cambridge, and University of Oxford. He was made Knight of the Academic Palms in 2008, Order of Chivalry of France for academics, a distinction bestowed by the French Ministry of Education. He is a member of the Academy of Management, European Group for Organizational Studies, Association of International Business, International Association for Research in Strategic Management, Strategic Management Society, and Transparency International. His research interests are deviance, fraud, and corruption, especially in emerging countries. He has published more than 50 academic articles.

Ambreen Waheed is the founding director of the Responsible Business Initiative, Pakistan's only citizen-sector enabler dedicated to responsible business and information communication technology. She is chair and co-founder of the South Asia Forum on Responsible Business. She has served on the Board Nominating Committee of Global Reporting Initiative (GRI), the Securities and Exchange Commission of Pakistan (SECP) Governance Taskforce, and the Board of Trustees, Asia-Pacific Roundtable on Sustainable Consumption & Production (APRSCP). She is a founding member of several CSR organizations and initiated the "Business Talk CSR" and "Living Global Compact Responsible Business" awards. She has taught at ESSEC (France), the University of Michigan (USA), and The Wharton School of the University of Pennsylvania (USA). She has a Masters in Computer Science and an MPhil in Management Science from the Judge Institute, Cambridge University.